*Routledge Revivals*

# Philosophy Without Metaphysics

Philosophy means 'love of wisdom,' but author Edmond Holmes fears the encroaching dominance of intellect over feeling. In this title, Holmes argues that metaphysics' reliance on intellect and pure reason undermines the study of philosophy. Rather, Holmes suggests a return to intuitional philosophy, combining thought and feeling. First published in 1930, this title will be ideal for students interested in Philosophy and Western Civilisation.

I0896281

# Philosophy Without Metaphysics

Edmond Holmes

Routledge
Taylor & Francis Group
ROUTLEDGE REVIVALS

First published in 1930
by George Allen & Unwin Ltd.

This edition first published in 2015 by Routledge
2 Park Square, Milton Park, Abingdon, Oxon, OX14 4RN
and by Routledge
711 Third Avenue, New York, NY 10017

*Routledge is an imprint of the Taylor & Francis Group, an informa business*



ISBN 13: 978-1-138-12592-6 (hbk)
ISBN 13: 978-1-315-64715-9 (ebk)
ISBN 13: 978-1-138-12597-1 (pbk)

# PHILOSOPHY WITHOUT METAPHYSICS

*By*

EDMOND HOLMES

"J'aime la philosophie et surtout la métaphysique ni quadrupède ni bipède, mais ailée et chantante."

JOUBERT

LONDON
GEORGE ALLEN & UNWIN LTD
MUSEUM STREET

FIRST PUBLISHED IN 1930



PRINTED IN GREAT BRITAIN BY
UNWIN BROTHERS LTD., WOKING

# CONTENTS



Two papers which appeared in recent numbers of the *Hibbert Journal* (October 1928 and October 1929) are included in this book, by the kind permission of the Hibbert Trustees and the Editor of the *Journal*.

# INTRODUCTION

My aim in writing this book has been to do something towards freeing Philosophy from bondage to Metaphysics. There was a time when Metaphysics dominated the pursuit of knowledge in all its branches. It arrested for centuries the progress of Physical Science. It made Medicine, which is the meeting-ground of many sciences, a murderous instead of a healing art. And it froze Theology, which in those days held Philosophy, Psychology and Ethics in solution, into the rigidity of "orthodox" dogma. It no longer dominates or even seriously influences Physical Science, which made rapid progress as soon as it was freed from metaphysical fetters. In Medicine, which has in large measure freed itself from its influence, it still lingers in the form of materialistic prejudice. Theology, so far as it is orthodox, is still held fast in its paralysing grasp. It still has something of a stranglehold on Psychology and Ethics. And it is still in the ascendant in Philosophy (its original headquarters), even the free-thinker, the agnostic and the sceptic being under its baneful influence.

How is Philosophy to rid itself of this incubus? By closing its door against it at the outset. For Metaphysics claims as its own the whole field of philosophical inquiry; and if its right to enter that field is conceded, its claim to monopolize the field will not be easily disallowed. Give it an inch and it will take an ell.

I deny that there is any place for Metaphysics in Philosophy. I do so on the ground that its fundamental assumption is a fundamental fallacy. What is essential in Metaphysics is its reliance on "intellect", "reason", "pure thought" to solve the master problems of Philosophy (and all derivative problems) by its own unaided effort, in entire disregard of the right of intuition to criticize, and of experience to test its conclusions. This blind reliance on intellect is the strength of Metaphysics for the time being, for it enables it to conciliate the "believer" by contemptuously ignoring the verdict of experience, and to conciliate the "rationalist" by contemptuously ignoring the criticism of intuition.

But what is its strength for the time being is its weakness in the long run. Divorced from intuition and experience, intellect can do no more, in its attempt "to understand the Universe", than reason deductively from its own "assumptions about reality". Its conclusions will therefore be worth no more than its initial assumptions. In other words, as providing a solution of the Supreme Problem, they will be worth nothing at all.

So far I have had in mind the *logical* metaphysics which Mediæval Europe inherited from Ancient Greece, and which dominated Western thought for many centuries. There is a school of speculative thought of more recent origin, which calls itself *empirical*, and which bases its system nominally on experience as such, really on an arbitrary limitation of the range of experience, which makes the issue of its thinking a foregone conclusion. This school, which is for the moment in the ascendant, identifies metaphysics with philosophy on one side and with science on the other. It may be doubted if it can make good its own claim to any one of these titles; but as it is avowedly metaphysical, and as it shares with logical metaphysics reliance on intellect for the solution of ultimate problems, it shall be made the subject of careful study. For it is its exclusive reliance on intellect which makes metaphysics so fatal an influence in philosophy; and whatever form that "faith unfaithful" may take, it must be regarded as inimical to the pursuit of ideal truth. What I deprecate in metaphysics is not its attempt to understand τὰ μέτα τὰ φύσικα, but its assumption that intellect, alone and unaided, is competent to unravel their mysteries, and the consequent assumption that in such matters mental satisfaction is attainable and is all that one need aim at.

There is a third branch of Metaphysics which must not be ignored. Intellect may go to popular thought (as expressed in popular belief or unbelief) for its premises, and reason deductively from these. In doing so, however abstruse may be its calculations and however far-fetched its conclusions, it will work under the ultimate control of popular thought. But popular thought means no more than the conscious thought of the average man. And it is not to the average man, as a conscious thinker, that one would go for the "wisdom" which philosophy loves and seeks. But it may fairly be contended that this branch of metaphysics makes up, in respect of importance, for its obvious inadequacy as a philosophy, by its wide diffusion in all ages and all lands.

The scheme of this book is in brief as follows: In the First Chapter I examine a typical metaphysical system of the Logical type. In the Second Chapter I examine a typical metaphysical system of the Empirical type. In the Third Chapter I examine two metaphysical systems which belong to the people rather than the schools: namely Supernaturalism and Materialism; and I pass on from these to Agnosticism, the philosophy of intellectual despair.

In the Fourth Chapter I plead for an alliance between thought and feeling, and for the task of "high thinking" being entrusted to the product of such an alliance—in a word to *Intuition*; and I go on to examine Intuitional Philosophy on its speculative (or poetical) and its practical side.

In the Conclusion I set forth what I, for one, conceive to be the creed of the intuitional philosopher.

# PHILOSOPHY WITHOUT METAPHYSICS

## CHAPTER I

## LOGICAL METAPHYSICS

PHILOSOPHY is "love of wisdom". Wisdom is the guiding light which shows us how to make the best of life. The fountain-head of wisdom is knowledge of reality. It is through experience that we gain knowledge of reality, learning, little by little, to distinguish higher from lower realities, or, in the language of dualism, reality from illusion. The philosopher seeks to gain wisdom by extending and deepening his knowledge of reality. And he seeks to extend and deepen his knowledge of reality by turning to account the various lessons of experience, by widening its range, by exploring its highways and byways, by acting on its hints, by following it into the depths of his own inner life.

In this work intellect plays an important but subordinate part. Its function is to discover and formulate such truth as can be presented for acceptance or rejection to the conscious mind. Hence it is most at home when it is dealing either (as in mathematics) with pure abstractions, in regard to which acceptance of certain premises carries with it acceptance of derivative conclusions, provided that the procedure of passing from premises to conclusions is correct; or (as in physical science) with material things, things which can be closely observed and freely experimented with, things which can be weighed and measured and otherwise accurately surveyed, and the relations of which to one another can therefore be determined with impartiality and precision.

It follows that if intellect is to achieve success, it must be content to work within comparatively narrow limits. Its indirect contributions to philosophy are of great value. By co-ordinating the data of experience and bringing order and unity into their chaos it makes the demand of experience for philosophical interpretation more insistent than it would otherwise be. Through the agency of Physical Science in general and of Applied Science in particular it progressively widens and deepens our conception of the material world, extends the range and makes more complex the subject-matter of experience, and so starts the mind on fresh adventures, provides fresh material for the exercise of its perceptive and critical powers, quickens its imagination and stimulates its desire for knowledge of reality, or, in other words, its love of wisdom. But the direct pursuit of wisdom is not for it.

The metaphysician thinks otherwise. He is not content to seek wisdom through an ever-widening and deepening experience. He wishes to present it to himself as formulated truth. The way of experience, as followed by philosophy, is too long and too circuitous for him. He demands "consummation and rest", and he believes that these can be achieved. In his attempt to get to the bedrock of thought and things two courses are open to him: he can dispense with experience and rely on intellect, in the sense of abstract thinking, for the solution of his problems. Or he can accept so much of experience as admits of a purely intellectual interpretation, and make this the foundation of his system of thought. In other words, there are two rival schools of metaphysical interpretation, the Logical and the Empirical. The former will be the theme of this chapter.[1] The latter of the next.

Let us see what a typical metaphysician of the Logical School has to say about his subject. "Metaphysics", says Bradley in *Appearance and Reality: A Metaphysical Essay*, which has been hailed as a masterpiece, "is an attempt to know reality as against mere appearance, or the study of first principles or ultimate truths, or again, the effort to comprehend the universe, not simply or by fragments, but somehow as a whole." This is a definition of philosophy, not of metaphysics. It

[1] It will be understood that when I use the word "metaphysician" in this chapter, I am thinking of the *logical* metaphysician only, except, of course, when the context makes it clear that I am using the word in a wider sense.

is possible to try to know reality, to study first principles, to try to comprehend the universe as a whole, by methods which are anything but metaphysical. Our author admits that it is possible "to reflect and ponder on ultimate truth—perhaps most of us do that—without being a metaphysician".

What, then, is it that differentiates metaphysics from other branches of philosophy? Not the desire "to think about and comprehend reality", but the desire to do the business of thinking "properly" and "strictly", in accordance with "the principles of thought's own distinctive working". The disbeliever in metaphysics, whose arguments Bradley is refuting, "permits the exercise of thought as long as it is entangled with other functions of our being, but as soon as it attempts a pure development of its own, he prohibits it forthwith". He does well to prohibit it when it undertakes to solve the riddle of the Universe. The word "thought" has a very wide range of meaning; and Bradley's restrictive use of the word is a potential begging of a very large question. Thought is nearly always "entangled with other functions of our being". We think feelingly, gropingly, broodingly, intuitively, imaginatively, subconsciously, practically. Except when our actions are purely automatic, there is something of thought, something of implicit reasoning, in each of them.

What, then, is the "pure development" of

thought of which Bradley speaks? What does he mean by the words "properly" and "strictly"? I presume that by thinking properly or strictly he means thinking *logically*, and that "the principles of thought's own distinctive working" by which the metaphysician is to be guided are those which are set forth in the authoritative treatises on logic. In other words, what Bradley has in mind is not thought as such, but conscious, intellectual thought—the thought which can follow the steps in its own processes, criticize these by reference to certain acknowledged principles, and present the results of its activity to the mind for deliberate acceptance or rejection. On the next page to that which I have been studying he defines "metaphysics as the intellectual effort to understand the universe". This definition is as true as it is concise, and I propose to take my stand on it.

Bradley claims the right to think "strictly"; but even thus early we can see that he does not think strictly enough. *Philosophy* and *metaphysics* are not, as he assumes, interchangeable terms. Nor are *thought* and *intellect*. Metaphysics is that branch of philosophy in which the effort to understand the universe, in other words to know reality, is purely intellectual. "Philosophy" is the *genus* of which "metaphysics" is a *species*; and "intellectual" is the *differentia* which distinguishes metaphysics from other species of philosophy.

And "intellectual" thinking is a species of the

genus "thought". What differentiates it from other species is the use that it makes of logic. What is logic? Before I begin to consider this question, let me call attention to a later passage in Bradley's book which throws a further light on the aim and method of metaphysics and which will play an important part in my attempt to interpret the principles and determine the limits of logic:

"Thinking is the attempt to satisfy a special impulse, and the attempt implies an assumption about reality. You may avoid the assumption so far as you decline to think, but if you sit down to the game there is only one way of playing." Did Bradley realize that in this sentence he had undermined the very foundations of metaphysics? The object of thinking (in the metaphysical sense of the word) is "to know reality"; and if "thinking" implies "as assumption about reality", which is binding on all who think, it is obvious that the metaphysical adventure is a farce and its issue a foregone conclusion. The starting-point is the goal. The assumption about reality with which the thinker begins his adventure will meet him, when he has done thinking, as the conclusion about reality to which he has worked his way. The significance of this undisguised "begging of the question" will disclose itself more clearly when we examine the (so-called) Laws of Thought.

And if you think at all, your thought *must* move in this vicious circle. "If you sit down to the game there is only one way of playing." Metaphysical thinking is a game. I welcome this admission. And if you sit down to a game you must abide by its rules. But the rules of a game are arbitrary and man-made, and are binding only on those who consent to play. They are not universally valid. They have not even any general significance. In a game one plays as a rule against an adversary, for the pleasure of playing and in the hope of winning. In metaphysics one plays a game of logical fence in the hope of defeating antagonists, actual or possible. But victory over a rival metaphysician is not the same thing as victory over the Guardians of the secret of the Universe. And the conclusions which the victorious metaphysician—and every metaphysician is victorious in his own eyes—claims to have established are in no way binding on "whatever gods may be". The attempt to think implies an assumption about reality; and that assumption determines the rules of the game; but it does not follow that it is true to the essential nature of reality.

And what do those who play the metaphysical game dispute about? That they do dispute is certain. The history of philosophy is the history of never-ending controversy. Why should this be so? The game has its own rules which all the players are supposed to observe. And those rules are determined by the assumption about reality which the playing of the game implies. What, then, is the bone of contention? I can only suppose that the different schools differ in their interpretation of the initial assumption about reality, and therefore in their interpretation of the rules of the game. But is not the assumption about reality "the conclusion", as well as the foundation, "of the whole matter"? And, if so, does not the game consist in the players trying to interpret its rules? But a game whose rules are necessarily and everlastingly in dispute is no game. It is a mere whirlpool of confusion and strife.

What is the "assumption about reality" which is implicit, according to Bradley, in the "attempt to think"? By thinking Bradley means *intellectual* thinking. We have seen that what differentiates this from other species of the genus *thought* is the use that it makes of *logic*. What is logic? I asked this question and then broke away from it. I will now try to answer it. Logic is the science or quasi-science which attempts to formulate and systematize the laws that govern the operations of intellectual thought. There are two main branches of logic, corresponding roughly to the two fields of mental activity in which intellect is most at home. Intellect is most entirely at home in Pure Mathematics, where the objects of thought are abstractions, and symbols take the place of words. There it is at its best, or at least its purest. The corresponding branch of logic is known as *Deductive*, the movements of thought which it surveys and directs being downward—from admitted or established premises of a general character to particular conclusions. Intellect is at its second best, so to speak, in Physical Science, where the objects of thought are material things which can be closely and accurately scrutinized, and where the terms used, though not mere symbols, are what is called *technical*, having as a rule a narrow and rigidly defined range of meaning, from which the emotional element is entirely excluded. The corresponding branch of logic is known as *Inductive*.[1] In it the mind proceeds from particulars to generals, from facts to laws. Its rules are less amenable than those of Deductive Logic to systematic exposition and authoritative formulation.

This is one reason why the "logical" metaphysician has no use for Inductive Logic. But there is another reason which lies deeper and counts for more. In Inductive Logic we start with experience and end with experience. Experience provides us with the premises from which we draw our conclusions; and experience provides us with the means of testing our conclusions. The validity of experience is (provisionally) taken for granted. No attempt is made to analyse it into its

[1] Induction, of a special kind, plays an important part in Mathematics; and deduction, of a more or less informal character, is freely resorted to in Physical Science; but on the whole there is more of deduction than of induction in Mathematics, and more of induction than of deduction in Physical Science.

constituent elements or to ask it for its credentials. It is for "pure thought" to do this. To determine the meaning and value of experience is one of the problems which the metaphysician attempts to solve. In his attempt to solve it he cannot well make use of the branch of logic which takes the validity of experience for granted. If his thought is to be "pure", if he is to think "strictly", "properly", logically, he must use as his instrument the other branch of logic, the branch which is known variously as *deductive*, *syllogistic*, *scholastic*, *formal*; the logic which makes internal consistency, correctness of procedure, conformity to its own rules, not conformity to experience, not ratification by sense-perception or (when this is unavailable) by intuitive conviction, the test of truth.

This branch of logic centres in certain (so-called) Laws of Thought. These laws are supposed to govern all intellectual processes. In inductive logic they remain in the background. In deductive logic they fill the greater part of the stage. They centre in what is called the Law of Contradiction. According to that law we cannot in the same breath both affirm and deny. The same thing cannot at the same time be both *A* and *not–A*. According to an associated law, the thing in question must be either *A* or *not–A*, and, according to another associated law, there can be no middle term between *A* and *not–A*.

Where, if anywhere, does this triune law hold

undisputed sway? In mathematics, where pure thought finds its most congenial field, the authority of the law is challenged and even undermined by the mysterious paradox of "Infinity". Parallel lines never meet. Parallel lines meet "at Infinity". These propositions seem to contradict each other; but both are true. In physical science the range of the law is so severely restricted by practical considerations of various kinds, by the need for accuracy in definition and measurement, by recognition of gradation in the processes and tendencies of Nature, by the operation of the law of relativity, by the counteracting influence of the logic of life and growth, that though there may be no overt rebellion against its authority its writ cannot be said to run far. In the ordinary everyday affairs of life the law holds good within limits, but as a harmless truism rather than a necessary truth. So far as it does receive conscious recognition it is (as we shall see) in imminent and deadly danger of being dualistically misinterpreted by popular thought.

Does the Law of Contradiction hold good when we are attempting the solution of ultimate problems? Does it suddenly acquire an authority so indisputable and so all-controlling that in the bare statement of it the solution of those problems is to be found? Is self-consistency the final proof of reality and truth? Is self-contradiction the final proof of unreality and untruth? *That the*

*Real does not and cannot contradict itself, that it always is itself*, is "the assumption about reality" which, according to metaphysicians of the "Absolute" school, "the attempt to think" implies. In this assumption Logic sets Metaphysics its master problem, and in setting it solves it. The paramount law of thought becomes the paramount law of things.

Are we to accept as conclusive this sudden and simple solution of the greatest of all problems? The logic of pure thought, the logic which centres in the Law of Contradiction, is the logic of Being, the logic of a static world. It takes for granted that things are as stationary as they seem to be to the careless or uninstructed eye. It was evolved before the idea of evolution had begun to dawn on human thought. And it is specially applicable to the material world, in which many things seem to stand still for long periods of time. But the world of our experience is a world of Becoming, not of Being. Pure Being, perfect self-consistency, is an idea of the human mind, an idea which, as far as we know, has no counterpart in objective reality. It is the foil to the idea of Becoming, the background against which the latter stands out and reveals itself to our thought. Or, again, it is the ideal goal of Becoming, the goal which the worldwide stream of Becoming is ever striving to reach, a goal which eternally attracts and eternally eludes. Or, once more, it is the sea into which the stream of Becoming is ever widening, a sea which is ever giving back what it receives, and which is therefore, though it seems to promise consummation, never self-consistent, never at rest.

The more deeply science penetrates the secrets of the Universe, the more successful is it in exposing the imposture of immobility, both as regards individual things and as regards the world as a whole. Things that seem, for years and even centuries, to be solid, stable, self-consistent, self-same, are found, when analysed, to be in a state of perpetual whirl and flux. Not a single atom in the outward world is at rest, in the sense of being free from internal commotion, even for the smallest imaginable fraction of a second. The electrons of which each atom is composed are ever revolving round their central orb, and the rapidity of their movements baffles imaginative thought. Now and again they even break away from their own orbits. All living things come under the Law of Growth, and growth involves perpetual change. The material world as a whole seems to come under the Law of Evolution; and evolution is growth writ large. And under the stress and the control of the Law of Evolution the world seems to be gradually spiritualizing itself; so that in the spiritual world, if we may provisionally distinguish it from the material, Becoming is not merely the paramount law of things, but the very essence of their being; for growth is of the essence of life, and it is through the further developments of growth that life rises to the level of spirituality.

What place is there for the Law of Contradiction in a world of Becoming? "The same thing cannot at the same time be both *A* and *not–A*." There is a pitfall in the words "at the same time". There is no self-sameness in time. Not for a millionth of a second does time stand still. Each millionth of a second is the negation of its predecessor and of all its predecessors. It is through perpetual self-negation that the course of things affirms itself. It is through perpetual self-negation that each living thing affirms itself. It is through perpetual change of identity that identity is established and preserved.

What is an oak-tree? Is it the acorn? The first green shoot that breaks through the clay? The sapling? The full-grown tree? Who can say? The growing plant is ever transcending itself, ever losing its identity, ever finding it. In each successive stage in its development it is, and it is not—itself. If it did not constantly disown itself, it could not remain true to itself. Its "ideality" is the mainspring of its life.

Bradley does not need to be reminded that we live in a world of Becoming. He goes out of his way to convince us that all the objects of our experience are

> "Shadow shapes that come and go."

In the earlier part of his book he examines many claimants to reality, and in each case the claim is summarily rejected, the claimant is turned down as an impostor, is told that it contradicts itself and that its boasted reality is therefore "mere appearance". There is no stability in the world, as Bradley sees it, no consistency, no self-sameness. Everywhere and in everything there is "ideality", a capacity for and tendency towards "self-transcendence"; and ideality is a conclusive proof of self-contradiction, unreality, untruth.

Where, then, is reality to be found? In "the Absolute"; in the world regarded as a self-contained "individuality", as a perfect, an infinite, an all-embracing, a self-consistent whole. This is "genuine reality". The phenomenal world, the world of Becoming, is "mere appearance". Because it is ever becoming, ever transcending itself, we know it to be unreal.

The dualism of the phenomenal world and the Absolute is, I think, the most false and futile that the mind of man has ever invented. And the most unpractical. Whenever a serious attempt is made to think it out, it breaks down and contradicts itself. Even when it is handled by Bradley, its ardent advocate, it makes demands on his philosophy which he cannot meet, except at the cost of disowning his own first principles. We shall presently see that appearance and reality, which in the earlier part of his book are mutually exclusive alternatives, become correlated opposites in the latter part—a transformation which undermines his fundamental assumption and wrecks the whole system of his thought. In spite of himself he cannot help seeing—the stress of his own subconscious thinking is too strong for him—that the world of appearances, in the course of its self-transcendence, *is becoming real*. But if there is gradation in reality, what becomes of the dualism of the phenomenal world and the Absolute?

Dualism, which ends by giving us two worlds instead of one, and transferring reality from each of the worlds to the gulf that separates them,[1] is the Nemesis of exclusive devotion to the logic of Being. The first thing which the Law of Contradiction demands from him who professes to obey it is that he shall distinguish between *negation* and *opposition*. The slightest departure from *A* is *not–A*. A book may cost 5s. or 4s. 11d., but the same book cannot at the same time and in the course of the same transaction cost both 5s. and 4s. 11d. 4s. 11d. is *not* the same as 5s., but it is in no way opposed to it. Negation in this case is entirely different from opposition.

Let us take another case. "The same statement cannot be both true and untrue." Here the Law of Contradiction may hold good, but it may not. If it is to hold good, the meaning of the word "true" must be rigorously defined. The statement

[1] See Chapter III, p. 120.

must either be one as to a matter of material fact or belong to an exact science. If it is a statement as to a matter of general interest—political, let us say, or ethical or æsthetic—the chances are that the Law of Contradiction does not apply to it. The chances are that the statement is both true and untrue; true from this point of view, untrue from that; true in some degree, untrue in some degree. When gradation and relativity come into play, the Law of Contradiction retires into the background. Truth and untruth may be mutually exclusive alternatives; but in the sphere of opinion they are, as a rule, correlated or polar opposites, each implying the other and drawing its meaning, in part at least, from the other, the two varying together in inverse proportion, while neither is ever met with in its ideal purity.

Language, as we know to our cost, abounds in pairs of antithetical terms, each of which stands for two correlated opposites. *Good* and *bad*, *high* and *low*, *large* and *small*, *wide* and *narrow*, *swift* and *slow*, *beautiful* and *ugly*—their name is Legion. To apply the Law of Contradiction, or either of its other selves, to correlated opposites—to say, for example, that every man is either good or bad, that every mountain is either high or low, that every work of art is either beautiful or ugly—is to talk sheer nonsense. But the temptation to talk such nonsense is very strong, and most of us succumb to it. The constitution of human speech is essentially dualistic. It cannot measure gradation except by the substitution, where that is possible, of symbols for words. It cannot, except by tiresome circumlocution, allow for relativity. Outside the limits of exact science dualism in speech, if not unavoidable, is very difficult to avoid. Yet we ought always to be on our guard against it, in the sense of not taking over-seriously the dualistic statements of ourselves and others. For the pity of it is that dualism in speech leads insensibly to dualism in thought, in feeling, in action. In the sphere of thought dualism is a fruitful source of error and confusion; in the sphere of feeling, of anger and hatred; in the sphere of action, of quarrels and wars.

In the ordinary affairs of life the confusion between negation and opposition is so common as to be almost unnoticeable. But one would have thought that the metaphysician, who prides himself on being strictly logical, would be on his guard against it. Yet nowhere is the temptation to think dualistically so overwhelmingly strong as in the sphere of abstract thought. For there, where we are dealing with our own ultimate, or at least ulterior, conceptions, where the terms that we use have a very wide range of meaning,[1] and

1 Where two words which seem to contradict each other have each a wide range of meaning, the normal relation between them, or rather between the ideas which they stand for, is pretty sure to be one of correlated opposition, not of negation. Where each has a world-wide range of meaning, they cannot afford to deny each

where the corrective influence of experience is wanting, there is too often but a single step from negation to diametrical opposition or even to entire annulment, and that step may well be taken before the thinker has time to realize what he has done or to what he has committed himself.

For example: The *existence* of a certain book on a certain shelf is in dispute. The book is or is not on that shelf. It cannot be both on it and not on it. Here the Law of Contradiction holds good. But here "existence" means no more than *is-ness*; and the slightest deviation from is-ness is negation. In that sense of the word there can be "no medium between existence and non-existence". The word has, however, another and a widely different meaning. When Fr. S. J. Hunter, S.J., tells us that "the creation of the substance of things must have been instantaneous because there is no medium between existence and non-existence",[1] he is using the word in that other sense. Existence for him means *Being*, a world-embracing and world-affirming conception; and non-existence means *non-Being*, a world-embracing and world-denying conception; so that between these two alternatives—for such they are in the eye of the logician—the whole world-process intervenes. The dualism of existence and non-existence has widened out in an instant, in obedience to the

other; they are bound to co-operate even while they oppose each other. If they did not, the world would fall in two.

[1] *Outlines of Dogmatic Theology*.

Law of Excluded Middle, into the dualism of Everything and Nothing.

We see from this example that there is a fatal and irremovable obstacle to the successful advance of pure thought into the field of philosophical speculation—namely, the fluidity, the Protean instability, of its terms. Pure thought is most at home in pure mathematics, where the terms used are *symbols*, which take the place both of words and things. In metaphysics the words that matter most, words that meet the thinker at every turn, are as far removed as it is possible to be from the status of mathematical symbols. Think of some of them: *soul*, *self*, *spirit*, *thought*, *feeling*, *will*, *happiness*, *goodness*, *truth*, *reality*, *world*, *universe*, *nature*, *God*. Will these, and the like of these, allow themselves to be degraded to the level of the alphabetical symbols of algebra or the diagrammatic symbols of geometry, so that pure thought, "guided by the principles of its own distinctive working", may be able to use them as counters in its speculative game? Have they not unfathomed depths and unexplored tracts of meaning, for the tentative apprehension of which are needed just those "functions of our being"—emotion, intuition, vision—from which thought must "disentangle" itself if it is "to attempt a pure development of its own"? Do not their meanings vary from age to age, from people to people, from person to person, from context to context? Are they not ever awaking trains of thought in every thinking mind, trains of feeling in every sensitive heart? Whatever pains the metaphysician may take to tie them down to the particular meanings which he may find it convenient to assign to them, they are too buoyant, too elusive, too much alive to submit to imprisonment in his—or any other—forms of thought. He has no choice but to use them in different senses, even at the risk of contradicting himself and so forfeiting his claim to the consistency which he regards as the one sure proof of reality and truth.

In Bradley's monumental work we have convincing evidence of the inability of pure thought to resist the pressure on it of the immense and ever-increasing vitality of language. We have seen that for him the Real is the Absolute, and that the phenomenal world, under all its aspects, is unreal. What is the relation of appearance to reality in his system? In the first half of his book the two are undoubtedly alternatives, mutually exclusive conceptions. What is unreal is "mere appearance". Now the word "mere" means "such and no more". If the word is used, as it seems to be by Bradley, of set purpose and with due regard to its meaning, it emphasizes the fact that the various aspects of the phenomenal world have in them no saving element of reality; in other words, that they are purely illusory. If this is so, there is no reality apart from the Absolute; there is no middle term between the "mere appearance", the phantasmagoria, of the phenomenal world and the "genuine" or true reality of the Absolute.

But in that case why use the words "mere" and "genuine"? If appearance and reality are mutually exclusive, if each is the negation of the other, the mere naming of each is surely sufficient to distinguish it from the other; and the words "mere" and "genuine" are therefore superfluous. But if the gulf between the phenomenal world and the Absolute is indeed impassable, how is the latter, in which all reality is concentrated, to be made available for human needs? How is the soul of man to be delivered from the toils of illusion?

When Bradley begins to ask himself this question, a change, profound and far-reaching, comes over the spirit of his philosophy. He realizes, for one thing, that the Absolute is beyond all relations, whereas "thought is relational and discursive, and if it ceases to be this it commits suicide". In order to escape from this deadlock, he allows thought to commit suicide and then resurrects it as a "higher unity", in which "*thought, feeling* and *volition* are blended into a whole". "This higher unity can find its Other in the Absolute." Pure thought could not do so without committing suicide. It is a pity that Bradley did not begin with this higher unity, *this critical effort of the whole man*, when he undertook to solve the greatest of all problems. To allow thought to undertake that task, to accept its solution as adequate, and then, when its inadequacy, *from the point of view of thought*, makes itself manifest, to call in "feeling" and "volition" (from which thought had been carefully dis-"entangled" at the outset), blend these with thought, and hand over to this "higher unity" the completion of the task which thought began, or rather the correction of the defects of the solution which it arrived at, was scarcely worthy of a serious thinker. Least of all was it worthy of the thinker who made inconsistency, self-contradiction, the one sure proof of unreality and untruth. If thought had need of feeling and volition at any stage in the process of thinking, it surely needed them most at the beginning. To disentangle thought "from other functions of man's being" was Bradley's initial mistake. The task which he set thought demands the co-operation of all man's higher power.

"Mere thought", which is, I presume, the same as pure thought, is identified in one passage with "one-sided experience". But one-sided experience is surely an inadequate base from which to set out on the greatest of all philosophical adventures. Can we wonder that the adventure, on Bradley's own showing, has proved a failure? The object of metaphysical speculation is to "know reality". To know reality is to know the Absolute, in which all reality is concentrated, and apart from which everything is "mere appearance". And to say, as Bradley does, that thought needs to be blended with feeling and will if it is to know the Absolute, is to admit that pure thought, on which logical metaphysics relies for its knowledge of the Absolute, has failed in the task which has been assigned to it.

Having undermined the foundations of metaphysics by exposing the inadequacy of disentangled thought as the instrument of metaphysical speculation, Bradley goes on to wreck his whole system by a tardy recognition of gradation in reality. In his use of such phrases as "mere appearance", "bare appearance", "genuine reality", "true reality", it is possible to see a faint foreshadowing of the idea of gradation, for if there is no gradation in reality, the qualifying words "mere", "bare", "genuine", "true" have no meaning. But, again, it is possible to see in Bradley's use of those words a resolute insistence on the strictly logical assumption that appearance and reality are mutually exclusive conceptions. It matters little which of these interpretations we adopt. What does matter is that, with the recognition of the idea of gradation, *appearance and reality cease to be alternatives and become correlated opposites.* The immense significance of this change seems to be lost on Bradley, but it cannot be too strongly insisted upon. It is a change from the logic of Being to the logic of Becoming, from the

Law of Contradiction to the Law of Polar Opposition, from oscillation between alternatives to the mutual interplay of correlated opposites. If there is gradation in reality, there is something of reality in all appearance, and something of appearance, in the sense of illusion, in all reality. The same thing is both real and unreal. It is and it is not—itself. According to the Law of Contradiction this identity of affirmation with negation, this flagrant inconsistency, ought to convict the thing in question of absolute unreality; but if there is gradation in reality, the thing is real as well as unreal. In other words, its partial reality, and its consequent disloyalty to the Law of Contradiction, afford convincing proof that it is absolutely unreal, that it is "mere appearance", pure illusion. The same thing can be both real and unreal, but it cannot be both partially real and absolutely unreal. Still less can it be absolutely unreal because it is partially real. In this glaring paradox, with its open mockery of our thought, in this refusal of the Law of Contradiction to co-operate with or to make any terms with the idea of gradation in reality, the philosophy of the Absolute founders and becomes a ruinous heap.

Let us see what the idea of gradation in reality involves. Before the idea dawned on Bradley's mind, appearance was one thing and reality another. Each negatived the other. Each excluded the other. Each was, as it were, complete in itself

—complete in its nothingness or complete in the fullness of its being. With the introduction of the idea of gradation a change came over their relations, which was not the less significant because Bradley never realized its significance. Henceforth each implied the other. Each owed its meaning to the other. Each drew its right to exist from the other. Each was always associated with the other. Neither existed in its own right. Neither was complete in itself. Each in turn, when abstracted from the other, became an ideal, eternally approachable, eternally elusive, lost in its own infinitude—the infinitude of Being or the inverted infinitude of non-Being. In other words, reality became the positive, appearance the negative pole of a process—the world process, for it was nothing less than this. It was to the co-operation of these correlated opposites that the phenomenal world owed its being, and the various objects of our experience their respective degrees of reality.

Looking upward along the ascending stages of reality one arrives at last at the idea of Ultimate Reality or Absolute Being. Looking downward, one arrives at last at the counter-idea of Ultimate Unreality or Absolute non-Being. These are ideas, not experiences. Each in turn passes beyond thought, beyond imagination, into a darkness which we cannot penetrate. For us reality and appearance always co-exist. They vary together in inverse proportion, but neither can wholly dissociate itself from the other. There is no appearance which is "mere" in the strict sense of that much-abused word, no appearance which has not reality in some sort and some degree behind it. And there is no reality which does not reveal itself, which does not appear, which does not clothe itself in form in some sort and some degree.

How does Bradley reconcile the idea of gradation in reality with his conception of the Absolute? When he introduced the idea into his philosophy he ought to have realized that the Law of Contradiction was no longer binding on him as a speculative thinker, and he ought to have revised his conception of Ultimate Reality. Had he done so we should have heard no more of the Absolute. For it was when appearance and reality (as he thought of them) were mutually exclusive alternatives, when each was the negation of the other, that he elaborated his conception of the Absolute, the dualism of the phenomenal world and the Absolute being but a reproduction in quasi-concrete form of the fundamental dualism of appearance and reality. But he could not bring himself to abandon a conception which was at the very heart of his whole system of thought. The idea of gradation in reality was an afterthought, forced upon him by the practical failure of his dualistic metaphysics, and instead of allowing it to revolutionize his philosophy, he so interpreted it as to bring it (as he imagined) into harmony with the central conception which it had in fact made untenable.

What conception had he formed of the Absolute? The Absolute, as he presents it to us, is "a single, all-containing individuality", a "system", perfect, real—real, in the fullest sense of the word, because it is self-contained and self-consistent, because it rests in itself, because it is entirely free from the taint of "ideality" or self-transcendence.

How does he know that it is "all-containing"? Because he thinks of it as such, is the real answer to this question. But it is not the answer which, as a metaphysician, he is content to give. He "inquires if there is anything which declines to take its place within the system of the Absolute", and satisfies himself that there is nothing. Of each thing in turn he reports that it *may* take its place in the "system", in the sense that there is no reason why it should not; and as, according to his general principle, it, like all other things, *must* take its place in the system, the conclusion is inevitable that it *does*. "What *may* be, if it also *must* be, assuredly *is*." Or, in other words, "what is possible, and what a general principle compels us to say must be, that assuredly *is*". Here we have *must* working under licence from *may*. And a very doubtful *may*; for, with his mind dominated by his "general principle", Bradley can scarcely be expected to deal impartially with the claim of this thing or that to fall outside the "system". Would it not have been better for him to take his stand firmly at the outset on his general principle and say that, since all things *must be* contained in the system of the Absolute, therefore they *are* contained in it?

But if the Absolute is "all-containing", and therefore super-infinite (if the word "all" has its full meaning), how can it be perfect? In the world of our experience there is imperfection on every plane of its being. And it is scarcely a paradox to say that it is well that this should be so. Perfection in human achievement is somehow felt to be a defect. And not without reason; for it is the proof either of a narrow range of activity or of an ambition which aims low. The perfection of maturity in living things is the sure precursor of incipient decay. And in the world as a whole, though there seems to be a general movement[1] towards a goal which we may perhaps think of as perfection, there is nothing to make us look forward to the goal being ever reached. Indeed, the very remoteness of the goal is, in a sense, the secret of its attractive force. Is the attribution of perfection to the Absolute anything more than a deduction from a metaphysical principle, from

[1] Bradley is careful to tell us that the Absolute does not move. No; nor does it do anything else. If we could think of it as doing anything or even as being anything, it would at once cease to be absolute. It cannot afford to enter into relation with anything, not even with human thought.

the "assumption about reality" with which, as we have seen, thought is armed when it enters the field of speculative inquiry? I doubt if it is. The arguments by which it is supported are scarcely convincing.

For example: in this world of ours evil is set against good and pain against pleasure. This is undeniable; but it does not disturb Bradley's complacent optimism. "Because the Absolute cannot contradict itself and does not suffer a division of idea from existence, it has therefore a balance of pleasure over pain. In every sense it is perfect." The existence of a balance of pleasure over pain is proved by an appeal, not to human experience, but to a metaphysical principle. And because there is a balance of pleasure over pain, therefore the Absolute is perfect. I cannot see the force of this argument. If the amount of pleasure in the world were represented by the number 5001, and the amount of pain by the number 4999, there would be a balance of 2 in favour of pleasure, as against a possible 10,000. I cannot see that so small a favourable balance constitutes perfection.

The truth is that the idea of perfection is one which the mind cannot, except by a metaphysical *tour de force*, apply to the Whole. Were it to do so, the idea would at once find itself in conflict with another idea, which is equally fundamental and inalienable, that of infinitude. It is in mathematics that pure thought (so far as thought can be pure) is in its happiest mood and does its best work. The "Infinity" of the mathematician is the analogue of the "Ultimate Reality" of the metaphysician. This will, I think, be admitted. And Bradley's name for Ultimate Reality is "the Absolute". That being so, it is instructive to note that "ideality" or "self-transcendence" is of the very essence of infinitude. The Infinite is that which eternally eludes us by eternally retiring into and beyond itself. May not one argue from this that self-transcendence is of the very essence of the Ultimately Real, and that the Absolute, with its suggestion of individuality, all-inclusiveness, self-consistency and perfection, is a misleading conception, involving a fundamentally false interpretation of reality? As the Infinite is "that which is beyond any assignable quantity"—eternally beyond, for it ever recedes as we approach it—so the Ultimately Real is that which is beyond any imaginable degree of reality. The Absolute is said to be self-consistent, all-inclusive, perfect. On the analogy of the Infinite the Ultimately Real is not self-consistent, for it has never found and will never find its real (i.e. ideal) self. It is not all-inclusive, for it is ever transcending itself and therefore ever extending its "all". It is not perfect, for it is ever advancing towards a higher perfection. What St. Catherine of Genoa said of herself applies, *mutatis mutandis*, to the universe: "From time to time I feel that many instincts are being consumed within me which before had appeared to be good and perfect; but when once they have been consumed I understand that they were bad and imperfect." What is it that consumes them? "Divine love" answers this question: "The higher up thou shalt go, however great a perfection thou mayst have, the higher will I ever stand above all to ruin all thy perfection." The idea of perfection is inseparable from that of completion and therefore of finiteness. In perfection a process is *carried through* to its conclusion, and there it stays and would fain rest. A perfect world is a self-contained world. There is in it no saving grace of self-transcendence. But perfection is not perfection if it is content with itself and stands still. If it cannot rise above itself it loses its perfection. The moment of final attainment is the moment of incipient failure. When high-water mark is reached the ebb has begun.

> "Things won are done; joy's soul lies in the doing."

When Bradley worked his way to the idea of gradation in reality, he ought, as I have said, to have revised his conception of Ultimate Reality. He ought to have realized that appearance and reality are correlated opposites, not alternatives, and therefore that the Ultimately Real is not an "individuality", not a "system", not "self-consistent", not "self-contained", not "perfect in all its details", but, on the contrary, is a self-transcending ideal lost in the darkness of its own infinitude. When a graduated process runs diameter-like through the heart of the world, its opposite ends are not limits, but poles, ideals—positive or negative—which pass beyond the range of experience, of thought, of imagination. And the interval between such and such a point on the ascending scale of the process, however relatively high that may be, and the positive pole is always infinite. When Bradley tries to reconcile the idea of gradation with that of perfection, the incongruity of the two ideas becomes apparent. He tells us that "the ultimate Reality, where all appearance as such is merged, is in the end the actual identity of idea and existence". In this formula the words "actual" and "in the end", with their suggestions of completion and finiteness, are significant. He goes on to tell us how gradation in reality is to be measured: "Throughout our world whatever is individual is more real and true, for it contains within its own limits a wider region of the Absolute and it possesses more intensely the type of self-sufficiency. Or, to put it otherwise, the interval between such an element and the Absolute is smaller. We should require less alteration, less destruction of its own special nature, in order to make the higher element completely real." We need not pause to ask what the word "individual" means in this context. What is significant in the passage is the twofold assumption: (1) that the various embodiments of reality in "our world" are separated from the Absolute by various measurable intervals—measurable, as is said elsewhere, by the "idea of perfect reality"; and (2) that by "alteration" this or that "element" or "principle", which is only partially real, can be made "completely real", can be made to attain to "actual perfection". This assumption involves a profound misinterpretation of the idea of infinitude. To speak of an "interval" between a subordinate element or principle and the Absolute is as though one should speak of an "interval" between a finite number and Infinity. If the interval is measurable, as it certainly is if the word "smaller" has any meaning, and if "alteration" can make what is partially real "completely real"—the Absolute is finite. There is no escape from this conclusion.

Try as he may to invest the Absolute with a comprehensiveness which transcends infinitude, the conditions under which our author thinks are too strong for him. The hybrid creation of his mind—hybrid because it is the offspring of feeling (though he does not realize this) as well as of thought—insists on clothing itself with limitations. Such phrases as "completely real", "actual perfection", "perfect Reality", "concrete Reality", though he may have uttered them carelessly and without fully realizing to what they committed him, betray the direction in which the central current of his thought is moving. Self-transcendence is of the very essence of infinitude, and self-transcendence is, for Bradley, the very proof of unreality. If the Absolute is infinite, it is ever passing beyond itself, ever advancing towards a higher perfection, ever becoming what it is not, ever contradicting itself, ever convicting itself of unreality. If, on the other hand, it is perfect and self-contained, if it is the last term in the ascending scale of reality, if there is nothing outside it, if it cannot transcend itself, it has achieved the finality which is the negation of infinitude. The two ideas —perfection and infinitude—may be forced by a metaphysical theory to dwell together in apparent amity within the sphere of abstract thought; but when freedom is restored to them by the working of the secret logic of the soul, they straightway fall apart, refuse to co-operate, refuse (one might almost say) to co-exist. And of the two it is perfection, not infinitude, which is of the inmost essence of the metaphysical Absolute. "The Absolute is perfect in all its details. It is equally good and true throughout."

We have seen that the Logic which is dominated by the Law of Contradiction and its satellites is the Logic of Being, not of Becoming. If Being could resolve itself into Becoming, if it could be realized that the inmost essence of Being *is* Becoming, the Law of Contradiction would cease to operate; for we should then understand that the world is for ever changing its identity, that at any given moment it both is and is not itself. The Logic of Being, with its demand for internal consistency, freezes the world into complete immobility, the immobility of "perfection"; and the Absolute, a word which suggests finality and rigidity, and therefore awakes no emotional response, is a fitting name for that still and silent world. But it is only in the sphere of abstract thought that the flow of the world-wide river can be arrested. The moment we descend into the world of experience, the world of feeling, of action, of life, the ice breaks up and the river resumes its flow. And in its flow it sweeps away all the assumptions, all the arguments, all the conclusions of the metaphysician, and places the deeper realities which he thought himself competent to investigate beyond the reach of his conscious thought.

The distinction between conscious and subconscious thought is one which he may not recognize, but which he cannot, if he would, ignore. In logical metaphysics the conscious workings of the mind are controlled by the Logic of Being, with its horror of self-contradiction and therefore of paradox, with its demand for consistency and its consequent banishment of imagination from the realm of speculative thought. But the subconscious workings of the mind are controlled by the Logic of Becoming, by the actual pressure of experience—of our daily, hourly experience of this living, moving, evolving, self-transcending world—of experience acting by secret methods of its own on the brooding rather than the thinking mind. Hence the inconsistencies in which the metaphysician is sure, sooner or later, to involve himself, inconsistency being, *on his own showing*, the final proof of unreality and untruth.

In the Preface to his book Bradley tells us that he came across the following sentence in one of his notebooks: "Metaphysics is the finding of bad reasons for what we believe upon instinct, but to find those reasons is no less an instinct." But surely if the reasons are bad one must reject them and seek better. And if the best of reasons are still bad, one must never "count oneself to have apprehended". There is a sentence in the same Preface in which the metaphysician is warned against taking himself over-seriously: "The metaphysician . . . like other men, forgets the narrow limitations of his own special province, and filled by his own poor inspiration, ascribes to it an importance not its due." These are wise words. Why did not their writer pay heed to them? As a typical metaphysician Bradley does undoubtedly take himself very seriously. He allows his mind to be dominated by his own arguments, and accepts as conclusive "reasons" which, as he reminds himself in a moment of illuminating candour, are necessarily "bad". Also, though he recognizes that his "special province" has "narrow limitations", he does not allow this obvious disability to deter him, *as a specialist*, from the attempt to solve the greatest of all problems, from the research of ultimate truth. On the contrary, he insists that for the research of ultimate truth specialization in metaphysics is indispensable: "To be in earnest in metaphysics is not the affair of perhaps one or two years, nor did anyone ever do anything with such a subject without giving himself to it." Nor does he find any place for *philosophical* speculation outside the "narrow limitations" of metaphysics: "So far as philosophy is religious . . . it has ceased, as such, any longer to be philosophy. . . . Its essence clearly must be confined to intellectual activity." The significance of this remark will become apparent when we remind ourselves that in his first chapter Bradley defined metaphysics as the "intellectual effort to understand the universe".

Is it not this insistence on the purely intellectual character of philosophy, this assumption that the research of ultimate truth must be carried on within the narrow limits of a "special province" of man's mental activity, which is responsible for the failure of metaphysics—I will not say to solve the problem that it sets itself, for the problem is insoluble, but—to accomplish a single stage in its journey towards its goal, or even to clear the ground for its adventure?

Let the metaphysician play his speculative

"game", if he will. The game will resolve itself, as we have seen, into an attempt to settle its own rules. But that need not deter him from playing it. A writer on Chess once said that a certain "opening" in that game was "one of the most stupendous achievements of the human intellect". Let the metaphysician say the same, if he will, of this or that metaphysical *tour de force*. But let him remember, in his intervals of self-detachment, that the game is a game, and that for the serious business of trying to understand the Universe is needed, not the specialization of any one mental function, but (I repeat) the co-operation of all man's higher powers.

CHAPTER II

# EMPIRICAL METAPHYSICS

Is there such a thing? Metaphysics may be defined as the attempt of intellect, divorced from emotion and spiritual intuition, to "know reality", to "understand the universe". Bradley, to whom we owe this definition, defines intellect (implicitly) as thought dis-"entangled" from "other functions of our being" and "attempting a pure development of its own", guided by "the principles of its own distinctive working". This definition severely restricts the range of metaphysics. Intellect, as so understood, works under licence from formal logic. The Law of Contradiction, with its associated laws, controls all its operations. Metaphysics, in this sense of the word, cannot be empirical; for it is one of the functions of pure thought to examine the credentials of experience as such, and to study the different kinds of experience, with a view to distinguishing reality from illusion in their respective contents. An empirical investigation of experience is necessarily inconclusive. It has no starting-point and arrives at no goal.

What place, then, is there in metaphysics for an empirical system? We can find a place for it only by using the word "intellect" more loosely than Bradley allowed himself to do. In physical science we see intellect, divorced from emotion and spiritual intuition, doing sound exploratory work and achieving cumulatively successful results, the value of which admits of being practically tested. The basis of its operations is acceptance of experience as trustworthy and revelational, as bringing the mind into contact with realities of various kinds. Through its analysis of the data of experience it penetrates into the heart of the world which it explores. But it makes no assumption as to the *status* of that world or of any of its subworlds. It leaves that question untouched. And the experience which it analyses with indisputable success is *sense-experience*; experience, through the bodily senses, of the outward and visible world. With emotional experience, intuitive experience, spiritual experience, supernormal experience, it has little or no concern. So far as it does concern itself with these it ceases to be strictly scientific.

Emulous of the achievements of physical science, thinkers who wish to know reality and so understand the universe, have asked themselves whether the empirical method which answers so well in the hands of the scientist could not be adopted by the metaphysician. In answer to this question the *New Realism* has come into being, and seems for the moment to be in the ascendant in the field of speculative thought. This has been the practical answer. But is it the right answer?

Are the foundations of the New Realism securely laid?

Philosophy, as I understand the word, is nothing if not empirical; for it is through experience that the spirit of man unfolds itself, and, as it unfolds itself, distils wisdom from its widening and deepening knowledge of reality. But I am using the word "experience" in its widest and deepest sense. I am not restricting its meaning, as physical science does, to sense-experience, to the contact with the world which we establish through our bodily senses. And I am entrusting the task of interpreting experience to emotion as well as to intellect, to intuition as well as to reason, to *judgment*—in a word, the judgment which is made possible by the co-operation of all man's higher powers. But empirical metaphysics, if it is to remain on an intellectual basis, must follow the lead of science in its attitude towards experience. It must leave untouched, at any rate in the initial stages of its inquiry, all experiences which are emotional, intuitive, spiritual and—above all—supernormal. For such experiences vary widely from man to man, from people to people, from age to age, and are therefore unamenable to a strictly intellectual treatment; whereas the data of the bodily senses, which are "constant and common, shared by all and perpetual in all", offer a fair field for the impartial, disinterested investigation which intellect, unbiased by emotion, is able to conduct. Physical phenomena are facts, in the sense that "what seems to all men *is*". They seem to all of us to be endowed with actuality, with objective being. It is with facts, not with dreams, or visions, or fancies, or fugitive feelings, or incommunicable experiences, that intellect begins, when it sets out, in the service of science, on the empirical quest of ultimate truth. And it is with facts that intellect must begin if it is to set out, in the service of metaphysics, on the empirical quest of ultimate reality.

Thus empirical metaphysics enters the field of speculative thought with an implicit assumption which must needs predetermine the issue of its inquiry. It assumes at the outset that analysis of sense-experience is the road to the fundamental reality which has its counterpart in ideal truth, and that what is ultimate in such analysis is self-existent, intrinsically real. This is how it interprets the universe at the beginning of its inquiry, and this is how it will interpret it at the end. It must confine its attention, at any rate while it is laying its own foundations, to sense-experience. Its exclusive reliance on intellect for the solution of its problems demands that it shall do this. But its pretension to the title of metaphysics demands that it shall invest the objects of sense-experience with a status which science, as science, has never claimed for them. The question of status, of intrinsic reality, counts for nothing in science proper. In metaphysics it is the thinker's first and last concern.

Such are the limitations which empirical metaphysics is bound by its own charter, so to speak, to impose upon itself. That we may the better realize how serious they are and how far-reaching are their consequences, let us study a typical system of empirical metaphysics. In Bradley's *Appearance and Reality* I studied a typical system of *a priori* or logical metaphysics. In Professor Alexander's *Space, Time and Deity* empirical metaphysics has found a thoughtful and courageous exponent. Let us see what he has to tell us as to the world in which we find ourselves.

He starts with certain sweeping assumptions, which are disputable, to say the least, but which, if one may judge from the light-hearted and almost casual way in which he formulates them, he seems to regard as self-evident truths. He begins by identifying philosophy with metaphysics. This assumption, which is pregnant with important consequences, is disputable, and I have elsewhere given my reasons for disputing it. Philosophy is the quest of wisdom, a quest which demands the co-operation of all man's higher powers. Metaphysics is at best a branch of philosophy, a branch which condemns itself to perpetual sterility, so far as its aim coincides with that of philosophy, by its blind reliance on intellect for the solution of the problems which philosophy investigates.

"But science", says the metaphysician, "relies on intellect for the solution of its problems, and solves them (within the limits which it imposes on itself) with undeniable success. Why may not metaphysics do the same?" Professor Alexander answers this question by assuming off-hand that metaphysics (alias "philosophy") is a branch of science. "Philosophy", he assures us, "is itself one of the sciences delimited from the others by its special subject-matter", and "its method will be, like theirs, empirical." He repeats this statement in various forms, but he makes no attempt to prove it. There is, however, a passage in the Introduction to his work, in which he betrays uneasiness as to the security of the foundations which he has laid. He is examining possible objections to his interpretation of experience and of the part that mind plays in it. "It would be a legitimate reply", he tells us, "to these remonstrances, that the existence apart from mind of the various groups of physical things and the existence of minds as one group among the existences of the world, as thus postulated by the empirical method, may be taken as a hypothesis for investigating reality. Without troubling our minds as to how things are related to our minds, or how we are ourselves related to our minds, let us make the assumption mentioned and see what comes of it. This is of the essence of the empirical method as a scientific method. You do not raise these questions in science. You assume the existence of life or matter, and you ask what it is. Let us in philosophy make the same assumption, and see whether in the end we do not get illumination as to our minds and knowledge."

Here our author touches on the very feature of scientific method which distinguishes it from the method which metaphysics, if it is to fulfil its self-imposed mission, ought to pursue. Metaphysics, to use our author's words, "investigates reality". Science does not. Science investigates phenomena. It accepts the physical world, the world of physical phenomena, a world of appearances, as worthy of investigation, and it proceeds to investigate it. It makes no assumption as to the reality of that world. Individual scientists, tempted by a quasi-professional prejudice in favour of their own subject-matter, may do so. Science as such does not. Science divides the world into subworlds, each of which has its own appropriate science or sub-science—the world of Space and Time; the world of "matter"; the worlds of life—plant life, animal life, human life, and so on. Corresponding to these worlds we have the main branches of science—mathematics, physics, chemistry, physiology, biology, psychology. No question is raised by science as to the status of these worlds. In the words of a distinguished scientist, "the truth we seek in science is the truth about an external world propounded as the theme of study, and is not bound up with any opinion as to the status of that world".[1]

The scientist is bound by his charter, so to speak, to ignore the question of status. The metaphysician is bound by his charter to consider it. And consider it he does, whether he intends to do so or not. The assumption that intellect is competent to interpret the universe is an assumption as to the status of that aspect of the universe which intellect is unquestionably competent to investigate. The assumption that metaphysics is a branch of science is an assumption as to the status of the physical world. Science does its work without let or hindrance because it abstains from raising the question of status. If a metaphysical system is to enjoy the same immunity from metaphysical criticism, it too must abstain from raising the question of status. But this it cannot do without forfeiting its charter and so ceasing to be metaphysical.

In adopting the phrase "empirical metaphysics", Professor Alexander commits himself to an examination of the credentials of experience. But the task is scarcely to his liking. His treatment of what is surely an all-important question is somewhat perfunctory. He seems to have an uneasy feeling that an empirical investigation of experience can lead to no certain conclusion. In the passage from his Introduction which I have

[1] *The Nature of the Physical Universe,* by Professor Eddington.

recently quoted he shows himself impatient of controversy, and claims that his work shall be judged, as the work of science is judged, by its results. But in making this claim he is himself fixing the standard by which the results of his work are to be judged. For he asks to be allowed to assume that his diagnosis of experience is correct. And this assumption will control the evolution of his system and determine the measure of its worth. When he has finished his work we shall have got exactly as much "illumination" from it "as to our minds and knowledge" as he has given us in his initial assumption.

What do we mean by experience? There are always two factors in it—a subject and an object. For the purpose of empirical metaphysics the subject of experience is of course the mind of man. Mind is a particular aspect of what we call spirit, or soul, or self. If the objects of experience are real things—and the empirical metaphysician must needs assume that they are—it is the percipient mind which guarantees their reality. So one instinctively assumes. But, for Professor Alexander, experience seems to guarantee its own validity, and in doing so to guarantee the reality of its objects. Where, then, does mind come in?

Before we can answer this question we must ask another. There are many kinds of experience. Of which kind is Professor Alexander thinking when he lays the foundations of his system of empirical metaphysics? His choice is, as we have seen, determined for him by his aim as a thinker. If he is to be both empirical and metaphysical, he must confine his attention to the kind of experience with which intellect, alone and unaided, is fully competent to deal. Of all the varieties of experience there is only one which satisfies this requirement—sense-experience, the experience which we gain through the exercise of our bodily senses, senses which are equally developed—or with variations which can easily be corrected—in all normal persons.[1]

The objects of sense-perception are what we call material things. They belong to the outward and visible world, by which we are surrounded, and which seems to us to be real. Science can analyse these things into impalpable elements; but it bases its analytical work on acceptance of them as phenomena, as things that "appear", and are of sufficient interest to us to be worth investigating. The scientist, as a scientist, does not raise the question of their reality; but as an ordinary man he is satisfied that they are at least provisionally real. At any rate, it is in dealing

[1] It is true that Professor Alexander recognizes the existence of a mode of apprehension which he calls "intuition", by which Space and Time and the primary or "categorical" qualities of things are apprehended; but he is careful to remind us that "primary qualities are apprehended by intuition through sensation", that intuition is "contained in sensation and masked by it", and that "*all* our experience is provoked through the sense-organs". (The italics are mine.)

with such things that intellect is most at home; and the empirical metaphysician has therefore no choice but to postulate their reality. Their genuine reality, whatever that may mean: provisional reality is not enough for him. He is satisfied, *in his own mind*, that the objects of sense-experience are real, and that through analysis of them lies the pathway to ultimate or intrinsic reality—the ideal object of his metaphysical quest. In other words, as the subject of experience, as one who perceives, thinks, knows—in a word as *mind*, he guarantees the reality of the objects of experience.

Does it not follow that the guarantor is in some sort more real than the objects of his guarantee; that his reality is at least of a higher order than theirs? To this question the empirical metaphysician answers No. He cannot afford to answer Yes. The objects of experience are for him real things—real enough to serve as the base of his metaphysical adventure. He knows at the outset of no higher reality. If mind were more real than the objects of its experience, he would have to explore it, in his quest of ultimate reality, instead of exploring the material world; and intellect, alone and unaided, would be unequal to so arduous a task. Mind, therefore, must be content to take its place among the objects of its own experience.

On this point Professor Alexander is emphatic.

He tells us that "the effect of the empirical method in metaphysics is severely and persistently to treat finite minds as one among the many forms of finite existence, having no privilege among them except such as it derives from its greater perfection of development". Is not this a case of putting the cart before the horse? The empirical method may necessitate a certain conception of mind. It by no means follows that that conception is true. The conception must justify itself to us on other grounds than that a certain metaphysical system requires us to accept it. No attempt is made to prove that the mind is but one of the many objects of its own experience. The nearest approach to an argument in support of this assumption is the statement that "the mind as an entity superior both to things and to passing states, is never experienced, and does not enter therefore into the view of an empirical metaphysics". This argument, if one may call it so, takes too much for granted. From the air of assurance with which it is advanced, one would imagine that it could not be challenged. But it can be. I for one am ready to challenge it. The mind, as an entity superior both to things and to passing states, is for me the only object of what I may call a self-certifying experience, the only object of experience which presents itself to me as intrinsically real. My experience clashes with Professor Alexander's, and flatly contradicts it.

Who shall arbitrate between us? I accept the experience of self-awareness as a revelation of reality—the revelation of self to self. Professor Alexander, having assumed at the outset that sense-experience is alone valid, and having satisfied himself that mind, as it presents itself to me (and to most men), is not the object of such experience, denies existence to it as a self-conscious entity, real in its own right, expels it from its "privileged position", and, regarding it as a dethroned usurper, relegates it to the humble position of one of the non-mental objects of its own "contemplative" experience.

But what is the value of an experience, the objects of which are real, but the subject of which, *quâ* subject, is an illusion? The duality of subject and object is of the very essence of experience. If either factor in the process is to be absorbed into the other, the object must be absorbed into the subject. For the subject is the guarantor of reality; and it may conceivably be able to raise the object to its own level by taking it up into itself. But if the subject, *quâ* subject, if mind *quâ* mind, *quâ* spirit, *quâ* self, is unreal, its guarantee becomes ineffective, and the objects of its guarantee, *with itself as one of them*, disappear into an evanescent mist of illusion. An experience which is real on its objective side only is no experience. It is as unreal, or rather as meaningless, as a one-sided equation.

But let us assume, for argument's sake, that mind has been justly punished for its past arrogance, that it has deservedly taken its place beside the non-mental objects of its own experience.[1] What then? Are we any nearer to a final solution of the problem of reality? I cannot see that we are. What does Professor Alexander mean by "reality"? He tells us in his Introduction that "in respect of being, or reality, all existents are on an equal footing". Here, in the two words "or reality", he solves to his own satisfaction the problem to which Bradley devoted 626 pages of closely reasoned argument. Thus do metaphysicians differ as to the rules of the metaphysical game! In his use of the word "reality" Professor Alexander exemplifies a tendency which seems to be characteristic of metaphysics as such, and which counts for so much in his exposition of his own system that I must turn aside to consider it—the tendency to play fast and loose with familiar words. Professor Alexander claims that metaphysics is a branch of science. He does nothing in his own treatise to substantiate this claim. From first to last he juggles with ideas which are more or less fantastic, paradoxical and elusive, and interprets words which are in common use in whatever way he may find convenient for the development of his train of thought.

[1] I will presently return to this theme. The dethronement of mind plays so vital a part in Professor Alexander's philosophy, that its challenge to one's instinctive convictions will not suffer itself to be long ignored.

The misuse of words in metaphysics takes two forms. Metaphysicians invent a jargon of their own, which they take quite seriously. Science too has a jargon of its own, which scientists take quite seriously. But in science the jargon is needed; it meets a genuine demand; and, within the limits which science as such imposes on itself, it does effective work. In metaphysics the use of a jargon is the outcome of a divergence from the broad highway of human thought and feeling into a by-way which will probably end in an *impasse*.

But the coining of pseudo-technical terms is a trifling offence compared with the deliberate misuse of familiar words, the open disregard of what I call their inherent meanings; and this is an offence of which the metaphysician, in his desire to follow out a particular line of thought, is often guilty. Either he puts his own interpretation on a word which is in common use, and so begs the question which is in dispute, or he stretches the meaning of the word to breaking-point and so turns its sense into nonsense.

By the inherent meaning of a word I mean the meaning which is the outcome of subtle movements of thought and feeling and experience (in the widest sense of the word) in many ages and many lands; which has been defined, more or less accurately, by centuries of usage; which reflects in its general trend the influence of countless associations; which has been insensibly modified by myriads of varying contexts; and which is charged, along the dominant stream of its own tendency, with potentialities of further development. The inherent meaning of a word, as so defined, cannot be lightly disregarded. It avenges itself on those who ignore it, in general by stultifying their arguments, and in particular by making them contradict themselves through its refusal to be ignored.

Professor Alexander identifies reality with being, in the sense of mere existence.[1] This is a misuse of words. If usage counts for anything, it must be admitted that the word "reality" is much more fully charged with meaning than the word "being". There is surely—to go no farther—a difference, in respect of reality, between dependent being and self-existent being. There is surely a difference, in respect of reality, between the "One" that "remains" and the "Many" that "change and pass". There is surely a difference between the antithesis of reality and unreality and the antithesis of being and non-being. There is surely some measure of meaning in the time-honoured contrast between "appearance" and "reality". Aristotle, whose authority in such

[1] The word "being" has two distinct meanings, or trends of meaning, which are too easily confounded. It may mean no more than mere existence, or *is-ness*. But, again, it may mean no less than the whole "substance of things", or *all-ness*. When Professor Alexander identifies "being" with "reality" he is using the word in the former sense. (See pp. 31, 32.)

matters carries weight, distinguished between "existing" and "existing *as fully as possible*"; and this is equivalent to a distinction between existence and reality. If

> "We are no other than a moving row
> Of magic shadow-shapes that come and go,"

it may be said that we exist, but it cannot be said that we exist as fully as possible, as fully, for example, as does the "Master of the Show". Professor Alexander tells us that "there are no degrees in truth and still less in reality". If this is so, why do we apply to "reality" such epithets as *ultimate*, *innermost*, *higher*, *supreme*, *transcendent*, *absolute*, *intrinsic*, *fundamental*, and the like? Professor Alexander finds it difficult to keep down to the level of his own crude dualism. He uses such phrases as "an ultimate reality", "perfectly and absolutely real", "relatively real", "the ultimate nature of reality", "primary reality", "fuller reality", "realities of a lower order". If there is no gradation in reality, if all "existents" are equally real, such expressions as these are a waste of words.

But let it be granted that all existents are real and equally real. What then? The problem of "appearance and reality" has ceased to trouble us. But a new problem, equally elusive and otherwise untractable, has taken its place. What is the criterion of existence, of "is-ness"? What does

Professor Alexander mean by "existents"? Objects of experience would, I presume, be his answer to this question. But there are many kinds of experience. Are they all equally trustworthy? And if not, why not?

Do the objects of mystical experience exist? Do the objects of clairvoyant sense-perception exist? Do the objects of prophetic vision exist? Do the objects of telepathic experience exist? Do the objects of the "varieties of religious experience" described by William James exist? Does the "next world" of the spiritualist exist? Does the "astral plane" of the occultist exist? Does the *aura*, the coloured emanation from a human being which some persons claim to be able to see and describe, exist?

Professor Alexander's attitude towards experiences which are abnormal in kind rather than in degree is dictated to him by the conception which he has formed of his mission. As an empirical metaphysician, he is bound to ignore, and in effect rule out, all the exceptional experiences which I have enumerated. He has in point of fact narrowed experience down to sense-experience, the sense-experience of the "standardized man"; and he could not well have done otherwise. But this involves a corresponding narrowing down of the universe. The denial of mind, *quâ* self, *quâ* spirit, real in its own right, which is seen to be a central feature of "empirical metaphysics", carries with it so many other denials that we need not look beyond it for the key to Professor Alexander's "science of being as such". For him the outward and visible world is the real world and the whole world. Reports of other worlds, of other planes of being, of other kinds of experience, must be dismissed as idle tales.

It is notoriously hard to prove a negative. A philosophy which is built on a basis of comprehensive negations rests on an insecure foundation which is liable at any moment to be undermined, with fatal results to the superincumbent structure. Towards the end of his book Professor Alexander makes the following significant admission: "If convincing experiment should in the future demonstrate the persistence of mind without its body which here subserves it, I should have to admit that the doctrine of this book would require radical alteration and, as far as I can judge at present, destruction." It is a pity that Professor Alexander did not study the evidence for survival before he elaborated a system of thought which a single proved case of survival would suffice to destroy. Had he made such a study the book might never have been written.

But the book has been written, and we must criticize it on other grounds than that it rules out a future life. The "real", as distinguished from the "notional", basis of the "New Realism" is belief in the intrinsic and exclusive reality of the material world.[1] The thinker who starts with this postulate will go on to look for ultimate reality in the elements into which matter is ultimately resolvable by scientific or quasi-scientific analysis. The physicist, when he pushes his analysis of matter to, or at least towards, its final limit, finds that matter dissolves under his hands into a "complex of metrical symbols", a "schedule of pointer-readings", and so forth. He is content that it should do this, for he makes no assumption as to the status of the object of his study. But his "ultimates" are useless for the metaphysician. The next step beyond them would take him into a world so unsubstantial as to be scarcely distinguishable from nothingness. Ultimate reality would come perilously near to being identical with ultimate unreality. "The modern scientific theories", says Professor Eddington, "have broken away from the common standpoint which identifies the real with the concrete." But empirical metaphysics, having started, in its attitude towards the material world, with acceptance of the common standpoint, has a prejudice in favour of the concrete, of which it cannot easily rid itself. And so it comes to pass that Professor Alexander, a typical exponent of the New Realism, diverging in his analysis of experience from the

[1] By the "material world" I mean the world which we look out upon, the outward and visible world, the world of sense-experience, the world with which we are so familiar that we cannot find the right name for it.

path of physical science, has gone straight to the two ideas which seem to be ultimate in popular thought when it contemplates the material world, the idea of Space and the idea of Time, invested these with objective, quasi-concrete being, and combined them (under the influence of the mathematical conception of Time as the fourth dimension of Space) in "indissoluble union", into an all-embracing whole, the one self-existent reality to which all our "empirical finites" "owe their being", and out of which the world of our experience is for ever "emerging".

Let us examine this conception. "The hypothesis of this (Professor Alexander's) book is that Space-Time is the stuff of which matter and all things are specifications." This is a bold, far-reaching and all-embracing assumption; and it obviously does not admit of proof. Professor Alexander takes great pains to elucidate it; and elucidation, in metaphysics, may be accepted as a substitute for proof. But does Professor Alexander elucidate his thesis, in the sense of throwing light on its inner meaning? I cannot think that he does. The truth is, as it seems to me, that his thesis has no inner meaning on which light can be thrown. You can get no more out of Space-Time than you put into it; and in like manner you can get no more out of the assumption which invests Space-Time with absolute reality than you put into it. As "matter and all things" are "specifications" of

Space-Time, so are all Professor Alexander's arguments "specifications" of his initial assumption. He does indeed present the assumption to us under many different forms. His statements and re-statements of it fill two bulky volumes. But they leave us where they found us. They do not carry conviction to one who is not already convinced. No amount of repetition can compel assent to a proposition which does not on other grounds command assent.

What do we know about Space-Time? Four-dimensional Space in which Time plays the part of the fourth dimension of Space is a mathematical conception. But mathematicians do not concern themselves with the problem of intrinsic reality, and there is no place in mathematics for the Space-Time of Professor Alexander's philosophy. Professor Eddington, who as a mathematician accepts the idea of four-dimensional space, and recognizes the existence of "frames of space-time", takes great pains to dissociate time from space. He "discerns", and would have us discern, "an absolute distinction between space-like and time-like separation of events—a distinction which justifies and explains our instinctive feeling that space and time are fundamentally different"; and he tells us that "events can stand to us in a temporal relation (absolutely past or future) or a spatial relation (absolutely elsewhere), but not in both".

For the empirical metaphysician experience—by which he means sense-experience—is the revealer of reality. What experience have we of Space-Time? We have experience of a kind—chiefly negative—of space. And we have experience of a kind—more positive and personal—of time. We have experience of space as emptiness, and of time as duration. Of Space-Time as a substantial reality of cosmic scope, of Space-Time as an indissoluble and all-embracing whole, of Space-Time as "the one stuff of which all things are made", we have no experience whatever.

Nor can we think rationally nor even coherently about it. We can think of it, through the medium of the conception of four-dimensional space, as the conclusion to a chain of mathematical reasoning. We can play with it as a metaphysical postulate, whose very extravagance, like that of a fairy-tale, makes matter-of-fact criticism of it seem out of place. But we cannot think seriously about its nature or its behaviour without losing ourselves in a fog of puzzles and contradictions. We are met at the outset by an obstacle which cannot be surmounted. We can think of time as succession in space. And we can think of space as enduring through time. But we cannot think of Space-Time as either *in* space or *in* time. A compound which is presumably indissoluble, and which is presented to us as all-embracing, cannot have its being within one of its own component parts. Can an apple-dumpling, in its indissoluble unity, get inside its own crust? Can Space-Time, in its indissoluble unity, have location in space or movement in time?

But if we cannot think coherently about Space-Time, perhaps Professor Alexander can. He professes to be able to do so; and he has in fact elaborated his thoughts about it into a complete "philosophy". What has he to tell us about this creation of his mind? Many things. Here are some of them: "Space and Time are, in their indissoluble union, the ultimate reals in their simplest and lowest form." Space-Time is "the primary reality". It is "the lowest of all stages". It is "the bare elements of the world". It is "the universe in its lowest expression". It is "the universe in its primordial form". This on the one hand. And on the other hand it is "the experiential Absolute". It is "the totality of all substances". It is "all existence and all substance". It is "the all-embracing stuff". All "existents" are "pieces" of Space-Time, or "bits" of Space-Time, or "modes" of Space-Time, or "specifications" of Space-Time. Or, again, they are so many "space-times".

Thus Space-Time is on the one hand the universe in its lowest expression, and on the other hand the universe in its totality. It is Alpha from one point of view, and Alpha and Omega from another. There is some confusion of thought in this. But it could not well have been avoided.

If the universe in its lowest expression is self-existent and intrinsically real, and if there is no gradation in reality—then, however much the universe may gain in complexity, it will never really rise above the level of its own lowest expression. It was Space-Time in the beginning of things, and it will be no more than Space-Time at the end.

But how does Space-Time—the primary reality, the lowest of all stages, the universe in its primordial form—transform itself into the world of our experience? In his attempt to answer this question Professor Alexander has recourse to various metaphors. These cluster for the most part round two ideas—the idea of Space-Time as a *matrix*, and the idea of Space-Time as *stuff*.

A *matrix* is a womb; and a womb contains embryos, potentialities which are waiting to be fertilized. How did the empty womb of Space-Time become full of possible existents? And by whom or what have they been fertilized? There is no answer to either question.

A *stuff* is a (more or less) raw material which has to be worked up into various finished articles. It has in itself no principle of self-transformation. Who or what has worked up, and is still working up, the stuff of Space-Time into the "empirical finites" which lie around us? There is no answer to this question.

How does Professor Alexander evolve the

universe out of the matrix of Space-Time? By making the matrix do what a matrix never does—*break up* into finites of ever-increasing complexity. He deals similarly with Space-Time as stuff. "Space-Time", he tells us, "is the stuff of which all existents are composed, and it breaks up of itself into these complexes within the one all-embracing stuff." How can a stuff, or raw material, break up into a multitude of finished articles? And, having done this, how can it remain "all-embracing"? Can a bowl break up into a multitude of fragments and yet remain the bowl that contains them all? In another passage Professor Alexander seems to regard "stuff" and "matrix" as interchangeable terms. He tells us that "Space and Time are as it were the stuff or matrix (or matrices) out of which things or events are made"; and he proceeds to make confusion worse confounded by saying that they are "the *medium* in which things are precipitated and crystallized". Elsewhere he tells us that "the universe consists of things which have developed within the one matrix of Space-Time". (Does the period of gestation last for ever?) And, again, that "within the all-embracing stuff of Space-Time the universe is an emergence in Time of successive levels of finite existence".

When metaphors which are used seriously and in good faith and in no spirit of paradox refuse to work, when they tangle up and obscure the thoughts that are behind them, we may safely conjecture that those thoughts are confused and self-contradictory, and that the mind of the thinker is moving in a wrong direction.

We are not in the least helped to an understanding of the universe by being told that Space-Time, whether as a matrix or a stuff, breaks up of itself into finites of ever-increasing complexity. We have no evidence whatever that Space-Time does anything of the kind, and we have no reason to believe that it can or will ever do it.

There is a gap, to go no farther, between Space-Time in its elementary bareness and the electron, or whatever else may prove to be ultimate in the physicist's analysis of matter—a gap which has not been filled up, and which, as far as we can see, will never be filled up. How is Space-Time to pass beyond that gap and so begin its work of world-building? It must *jump* the gap. No other course is open to it. And, having jumped that gap, it will have to jump more gaps.

This is the weakness of the "New Realism", that when, in his quest of reality, the thinker has resolved, by "analysing it to the death", the familiar world into what he regards as its ultimate elements, he can make no use of these. If he could use them constructively, as Science, when "Applied", uses its ultimates or penultimates, if he could take them and out of them build up, if only in thought, a new world, "remoulding" the old "to his heart's desire", he would not have laboured in vain. But he cannot do this. What can he do, then, but reverse the process of analysis, make its goal his starting-point and its starting-point his goal; in other words, on the foundations to which he has dug down build up in successive stages—electrical (shall we say?) material, vital, mental—the world of "empirical finites" in which we live and move and have our being? He began by accepting that world as intrinsically real, as being in itself what it seems to be to his perceptive faculties, and his analysis of it has added nothing to its reality. A synthetic philosophy, which tries, by imaginative insight, to discern the real in and beyond the apparent—in other words, which identifies the real with the ideal—may be creative in theory and so prepare the way for creation in practice. A philosophy which is "analytical to the death" is doomed, self-doomed, to perpetual sterility.

I have touched incidentally on what seems to be a central feature of empirical metaphysics—its attribution of absolute validity to the sense-experience of the "standardized man". This is the necessary counterpart of the assumption which dominates that philosophy—that the world of our experience is intrinsically real. But it cuts two ways. It provides for the glorification of what is ultimate in our analysis of the material world—in Professor Alexander's case, of Space-Time; but in doing so, it also provides, as we shall now see, for the rehabilitation of *mind.*

Professor Alexander tells us that "Space-Time is absolute and independent of the observer". Who or what guarantees its absoluteness? The mind of Professor Alexander. For there is nothing absolute in this world of ours "but thinking makes it so". And thinking is done by mind. If the Absolute could announce itself to us as such, its message would have to be received by mind, and mind would have to satisfy itself as to the genuineness of the message and the authenticity of its source.

But let us follow Professor Alexander in his attempt to present to us a world which is real in itself and independent of mind. We have seen that a jump—a prodigiously long jump—takes him from Space-Time to *matter.* Another jump will take him from matter to *life.* A third jump will take him from life to *mind.* Let us pause there for the moment. Corresponding to each jump on the part of Professor Alexander there is an "emergence" on the part of the evolving world. Matter is an "emergent" from Space-Time, or perhaps from some intermediate level of being which has not yet been determined. Life is an emergent from matter. Mind is an emergent from life. When Space-Time is no more than bare Space-Time, it is endowed with certain qualities which Professor Alexander calls *a priori,* or "categorical", or *primary*. When it becomes matter it is endowed with a new set of qualities which he calls *secondary*. When it becomes mind it is endowed with a third set of qualities which he calls *tertiary*.

Now it is the earnest conviction of Professor Alexander that the primary and secondary qualities are inherent in Space-Time as it passes through its various stages, that they are intrinsically real, that they owe nothing to mind. This is equivalent to saying that the world which is clothed in these qualities is in itself what it seems to be to the perceptive and apprehensive mind; and this again is equivalent to saying that mind, through the senses, is competent to see the world as it really is. This is surely a great concession on the part of Professor Alexander. For even if it does not involve the restoration of mind to the throne from which it has been expelled, it does undoubtedly involve the exaltation of it to a "privileged position". But I will not, for the moment, press this point.

Let us examine the qualities which are said to be inherent in Space-Time, both in itself and in its various manifestations, and let us see if Professor Alexander can make good his contention that they are "wholly independent of the observer", that is, of mind.

The primary qualities—substance, causality, identity, universality, particularity and the rest—

differ from the secondary qualities in being predicable of all "existents", in being "all-pervasive", or, as Professor Alexander would say, in being inherent in Space-Time as such. According to one school of thought they are ways of looking at things, or thinking about things, which mind brings with it to the contemplation of its objects. They are undoubtedly ideas of the human mind; but, according to Professor Alexander, the ideas are in the mind because the things for which they stand are outside the mind, essential aspects of Space-Time as such. *Substance*, for example, is "a specially defined volume of Space-Time". "The self-*identity* of a thing is its occupation of a space-time." "*Causality* is the relation of continuity between two different motions" ("motion" being another name for Space-Time). And so on. Mind has nothing to say to the primary qualities except to apprehend them through the medium of the perceptive faculty which he calls "intuition", a faculty which (as we have seen) "precedes all sensation, but only in the sense that it is contained in sensation and masked by it".

Professor Alexander makes no attempt to defend his position. In dealing with this, as with other contentious matters, he seems to think that dogmatic statement needs no other support than that of frequent repetition. Given enough of the latter, the statement is self-proved.

But the subjective element in the primary

qualities is not to be got rid of quite so easily as Professor Alexander assumes. Let us take the idea of *causality* and apply it to a concrete case. A ship is lost at sea. What was the cause of the disaster? The violence of a gale might be one answer to this question. The carelessness of a pilot, another. The state of the tide, a third. The impatience of the captain, a fourth. The untrustworthiness of a chart, a fifth. The breakdown of the engines, a sixth. Here are six answers to our question, any one of which might be accepted as correct if it happened to give the inquirer, with his particular object in view, mental satisfaction. The cause of a thing has been duly set forth—not absolutely, of course, but relatively and provisionally—when the mind of the inquirer rests in the account given. The search for cause resolves itself into the search for mental satisfaction. In the case of a shipwreck the engineer would have one point of view, the calculator of tides another, the cartographer a third, and so on. An exhaustive inquiry would take account of all the causes enumerated, and would no doubt in the course of its investigation unearth many more. But from first to last it would be a demand for mental satisfaction, a demand for an account of the disaster in which mind—mind *as such*, one might almost say—could *rest*.

Does Professor Alexander seriously believe that his formula would prove adequate in such a case as this? He tells us that causality is "the relation of continuity between two different motions". Another thinker might say, with at least equal show of reason, that causality is the projection into the world around us of an inner experience, the experience of one's own power of initiating action, of getting things going. Statements about the primary qualities can neither be proved nor disproved. They are therefore eminently suitable for metaphysicians to dispute about. Let us leave them in their hands.

What of the secondary qualities—colour, sound, scent, savour, and the various qualities which the sense of touch makes known to us? Surely the percipient mind plays some part in the production of these. Physicists whose judgment carries weight assure us that it plays a leading part. Professor Eddington, for example, in the Introduction to his work *The Nature of the Physical World*, contrasting the familiar external world with "the external world of physics", tells us that the latter "has become a world of shadows", and goes on to say, "It is all symbolic, and as a symbol the physicist leaves it. Then comes the alchemist Mind who transmutes the symbols. The sparsely spread nuclei of electric force become a tangible solid; their restless agitation becomes the warmth of summer; the octave of æthereal vibrations becomes a gorgeous rainbow." Elsewhere, speaking of "colour in the familiar world and its counterpart electro-magnetic wave-length in the scientific world", he says: "Hence we have little hesitation in describing the waves as objective and the colour as subjective. The wave is the reality[1] or the nearest we can get to a description of reality; the colour is mere mind-spinning. The beautiful hues which flood our consciousness under stimulation of the waves have no relevance to the objective reality."

Thus Professor Eddington. But Professor Alexander, faithful to his self-imposed mission of belittling mind *ad majorem Spatii-Temporis gloriam*, denies to it any share in weaving the vesture of the familiar world. If grass seems to be green, the reason is that it *is* green. If bluebells seem to be blue, the reason is that they *are* blue. If a rock seems to be hard, the reason is that it *is* hard. If sugar seems to be sweet, the reason is that it *is* sweet. And so on. The secondary qualities are all strictly objective. Mind has nothing to do with them except to apprehend them through sense-perception.

When doctors disagree, who shall decide? I am in entire agreement with Professor Eddington. But I am neither a physical nor a metaphysical expert. And so, if I am to intervene in this quarrel, I must content myself with asking Pro-

[1] Here the meaning of the word "reality" is obviously determined by its context. When Professor Eddington, in a later chapter, deals with the problem of Reality, he uses the word in a wider and deeper sense.

fessor Alexander one or two simple and fairly obvious questions: Is there such a thing as "blue distance"? Are there any

"blue hills that are really blue"?

Is "the blue Mediterranean" really blue? Is the sky on a summer day really blue? Are the glorious colours of a sunset really there (wherever "there" may be)? The answer to these questions is, I presume, in each case, *No.* One must not stand too far away from the things which one contemplates. But on the other hand one must not stand too near to them. One must not pry into them too closely. For the "standardized man" snow is undoubtedly white. But if we pry into it, we find that it is composed of crystals of transparent ice. At what precise distance, then, is one to stand from an object in order to see it as it really is? If, by changing one's position, one can change the appearances of things, the part that mind plays in perception cannot be wholly passive.

Let us pass on to the tertiary qualities. In regard to these Professor Alexander makes an admission which undermines the foundations of his philosophy so effectively as to imperil the security of the whole structure. He insists that "the tertiary qualities" (or "values", as he sometimes calls them) "are as real as the primary or secondary"; but he adds that "unlike the empirical qualities of external things they imply the amalgamation of the object with the human appreciation of it". They imply more than this. We are told in another passage that "the tertiary qualities, truth and goodness and beauty, though they differ from the primary or secondary ones in being creations of mind, are not the less real. Their dependence on the mind does not deprive them of reality. . . . The mind is the highest empirical finite we know. Strange that its touch should be thought to de-realize its creations".

"Creations of mind"; of mind, which is no more than "a set of events occurring in the body"; of mind, whose psychoses are all neuroses; of mind, which "has neither life nor energy"; of mind, which is "one among many forms of finite existence, having no privilege among them except what it owes to its greater perfection of development". How can this be? We are expressly told that Space-Time, which includes all things and is all things, is "absolute and independent of the observer"; that the objects of our experience owe nothing to the percipient mind, and so on. That mind—dethroned and degraded, expelled from the privileged position which it had usurped, lowered to the level of the non-mental objects of its own experience—should suddenly become creative, not in any metaphorical sense of the word, but in the sense that the highest qualities known to us owe to it their reality and their very being—this is surely one of the strangest of all the transformation-scenes in the kaleidoscopic drama of metaphysical speculation!

And the more closely we examine it the stranger does it become. Let us take the case of *beauty*. "In the beautiful object," says Professor Alexander, "whether of art or nature, one part is contributed by the mind. The beautiful owes some part of its meaning to the mind, and so far it owes to the mind, not only its *percipi* as every perceived object does, but its *esse*." Now one of the chief factors in the production of beauty is *colour*. In what relation does colour stand to mind? Science analyses colour into electro-magnetic waves. To the percipient mind these waves present themselves as the various colours. To what is the transformation of waves into colour due? Professor Alexander will not allow that it is due in any respect or degree to the interpretative action of mind. For him the colours are purely objective. Mind perceives things as red, blue, yellow, etc., because the objects of its perception *are* red, blue, yellow, etc. "If colour were, as it is alleged to be, the creation of mind, we should have the unintelligible result that a set of vibrations is seen not as vibrations, but as colour."[1] The part that mind plays in perceiving colour is purely passive and receptive. But what if the colour happens to be beautiful? According to

[1] But the set of vibrations *is* seen, not as vibrations, but as colour. This may be "unintelligible", but is certainly undeniable.

Professor Alexander, the mind then ceases to be passive, and becomes not active only but creative. The beauty of the electro-magnetic waves is a creation of mind. But surely the translation of the waves into beauty is a far higher achievement than the translation of the waves into colour. And if mind can perform the more difficult feat, why should it be thought incredible that it can perform the easier?

But if mind can perform the easier feat, if it can translate certain vibrations into colour and others into sound, where, in our search for what is purely objective, "absolute and independent of mind", will this unweaving of the vesture of Nature stop?

I will not attempt to answer this question, but I will ask another. Given that mind can create the tertiary qualities, in what sense can it be said to endow them with reality? Professor Alexander claims that they are objectively real.[1] Can this

[1] Professor Alexander does not seem to be quite easy in his mind as to the reality of beauty. He reminds us that he who sees a work of nature or of art as beautiful sees it "incorrectly". "Considered from the point of view of cognition, the beautiful object is illusory, for it does not as an external reality possess the characters which it possesses for the æsthetic sense." His faith in the intrinsic reality of the external world is touching. No thinker has ever striven so earnestly to de-subjectify himself, to subordinate reality to objectivity. (He has even convinced himself that pleasure and pain are objective, not subjective!) But is not æsthetic appreciation a higher kind of cognition? Who can be said to see a stately beech-tree as it really is—the artist who admires its beauty or the woodman who measures it in his mind's eye and sees it as so many feet of timber, so many logs of firewood, so many loads of brushwood?

claim be sustained? Beliefs, opinions, æsthetic tastes, standards of right and wrong, vary widely from age to age, from race to race, from country to country, from man to man. Architecture, decoration, furniture which are thought beautiful in one age, fall into disrepute in another, and may come into their own again in a third. Scenery which enchants one man makes no appeal to another. Murder is reprobated in most countries; but there are countries in which it is thought morally wrong not to carry on a blood-feud. Opinions—ethical, political, economical, sociological—which pass as correct to-day will be called in question to-morrow and discarded the day after: the orthodoxies of one generation are the heresies of another. And so on.

What, then, is to be the test of reality when we are considering the tertiary qualities of things? "So far as a man is good", says Professor Alexander, "he embodies the common judgment, he is the wise man of Aristotle, or he is the standardized man." "A mind which judges truly is one which judges coherently with the judging of other minds. Truth implies possession by a standard mind." It is the same, I presume, with beauty. That is beautiful which is judged to be so by the man of correct taste, the "standardized man" in the sphere of æsthetic values. Now it is safe to appeal to the standardized man as against the colour-blind man, the man who is hard of hearing, the man whose sense of smell or of taste is defective. But is it safe to appeal to him as against the saint, the prophet, the sage, the poet, the creative artist? Was Christ a standardized man? Was Buddha? Was Plato? Was Shakespeare? Was Michelangelo? In creating the tertiary qualities mind seems to be calling into being a new, an ideal world. If this is so, then the tertiary qualities owe their reality, not to their endorsement by the standardized man, but to the ideality which is at the heart of them and which is the supreme principle of unity in their infinite diversity.[1]

So much for the Qualities. Let us now go back to the problem of Emergence. We are living in an emergent world. Let this be granted. Two questions at once arise. Out of what is the world emerging? And why is it emerging? Professor Alexander knows the answers to these questions. No one else does. The world is emerging out of Space-Time. And the reason why it is emerging is that there is in Space-Time a *nisus*, a sustained effort, which makes for emergence. If Professor Alexander is satisfied with these answers I do not grudge him his satisfaction. The first answer is a fantastic assumption. The second is about as convincing as the well-known answer to the question, Why does opium send one to sleep? Because it has a sleep-producing virtue.

[1] Is it not Brahma who says in one of the Upanishads, "I am beauty itself among beautiful things"?

But in any case the world *is* emerging. The whence and the why of its emergence may be unknown; but the steps in the process of emergence can be traced. We have already traced them, in Professor Alexander's company—for here he is on safe ground—as far as mind. The successive stages are *matter*, *life*, and conscious life, or *mind*. What comes next to mind? Here, as it seems to me, Professor Alexander deliberately goes astray. His answer is *deity*. The right answer is "*self-conscious mind, or spirit*".

Professor Alexander has no use for spirit. He seldom mentions the word. There is a passage towards the end of his book in which he warns us against identifying deity with spirit. Apart from this he virtually ignores it. The truth is that, as a claimant to reality, spirit is a formidable rival to Space-Time. It gives us, if we accept its self-revelation, a new test and a new measure of reality. For the empirical metaphysician reality is the objective counterpart of sense-experience. In self-consciousness, in the revelation of spirit to spirit, of self to self, sense-experience, as the revealer of reality, is transcended and superseded. The experience of self-consciousness is self-certifying. For spirit, which reveals itself to itself, which is at once subject and object, shines by its own light and guarantees its own reality.

What can Professor Alexander do, then, if he is to safeguard the intrinsic reality of Space-Time, but reject the experience of self-consciousness and so convict the rival claimant of imposture? He is bound in any case to reject it. For in his philosophy sense-experience is the only revealer of reality; and it is not through the senses that I know, and am known to, myself.

He assures me that "the mind as an entity superior both to things and to its own mental states is never experienced". I have already met this statement with point-blank contradiction. He repeats it in many forms; but in whatever form he may repeat it, I will meet it with point-blank contradiction. My experience clashes with his; and my experience is not invalidated in the slightest degree by his dogmatic limitation of experience to sense-experience, a limitation which is wholly arbitary, and against which experience, in the larger and deeper sense of the word, unceasingly protests.

And I am not alone in my acceptance of self-consciousness as a genuine experience and a revealer of reality. When Professor Eddington says, "I very much doubt if any one of us has the faintest idea of what is meant by the reality or existence of anything but our own Ego" . . . "I know that I think with a certainty which I cannot attribute to any of my physicist knowledge of the world." . . . "Mind is the first and most direct thing in our experience, and all else is remote inference"; he is giving forcible expression to feelings which are, I believe, shared by most thoughtful men, men who are able to think disinterestedly because they have no metaphysical axes to grind. The eminent psychologist, William James, speaks to the same general effect when he tells us (with reference to the inner life of the spirit) that "the inner recesses of feeling, the darker, blinder strata of character, are the only places in the world in which we catch real facts in the making and directly perceive how events happen and how work is being actually done"; and when he says (in his analysis of experience) that "the inner state is our very experience itself, its reality and that of our experience are one".

Professor Alexander assures me that though I can never "contemplate" myself, I can and do and must "enjoy" myself. Let me assure him on the contrary that though I can and do and must "contemplate" myself, I do not often "enjoy" myself. The word "enjoy" applied, as he applies it, to a permanent mental state, is so inappropriate and yet so necessary for his purpose, that I cannot but think that the purpose—the denial of validity to self-consciousness as an experience, without wholly denying self—is at fault.

Empirical metaphysics, as expounded by Professor Alexander, seems to me to turn the real order of things upside down. The ascription of ultimate reality to the ultimate elements of things, whether these be atoms, or electrons, or the "pointer-readings" of the mathematician, or the Space-Time of Professor Alexander, will have one inevitable result. As we follow the world in its ascent from the first beginnings of things to the present stage in its development, we shall find that there is a constant tendency for each stage in turn to drag the stage next above it down to its own level, and to sink to the level of the stage next below it.

This is equivalent to saying that the one fundamental reality, as it ascends from level to level, tends to shed something of its reality, its presumed inability to make further gain—for what is absolute cannot transcend itself—turning at last to actual loss. More especially is this the case when it passes, in its ascent, beyond the limits of sense-experience. When we are told, for example, that mind is "a set of events occurring in the body and principally in the brain", that "the mental process and the neural process are one and the same existence", that "the mind is equivalent to the totality of certain neural processes as they are enjoyed", we instinctively feel that for him who says these things the brain, with its 14,000,000,000 neurons, the brain which can be seen, touched, handled, dissected, is the substance, and the mind the shadow, the brain the solid actuality, the mind an empty name.

This tendency to drag back higher to lower levels of existence gives rise to reckless departures from usage in the use of familiar words—a characteristic feature of the empirical philosophy on which I have already commented and which alone, as it seems to me, suffices to discredit it. Words which are applicable to the higher levels, which have their established meanings by reference to these, are transferred, by a stretching of their meanings, to lower levels, till at last breaking-point is reached, and what is supposed to be sense becomes sheer nonsense. The words "mind" and "knowledge", which properly belong to the level of conscious life, are applied to the lower levels, and at last to the lowest of all. We are told, for example, that "a secondary quality is the mind of its primary quality"; that "knowing may be used in an extended sense for the relation between any finite and those of lower order"; that "the material floor is assured of the materiality of the table"; that "in Space-Time the instant performs to the point the office of mind"; that "point-instants have conscious enjoyment and assurance"; that the "monad" (point-instant) "has an intimate first-hand and perfect knowledge of the world".

We are told, again, *deity* being the next higher level to mind, that "for any level of existence deity is the next higher level"; that "for creations possessing only the primary qualities—their god was matter"; that "God's deity is the issue in Time of a tendency or *nisus* in the world . . . an issue which is dependent on the nature of things lower than itself"; that "God's deity depends on mind, and this in turn on finites of a lower order, until ultimately we reach the simple matrix of Space-Time"; that "God's distinctive character of deity is not creative but created"; that "God is an infinite creation of the universe of Space-Time".

A system of thought which cannot express itself except by turning the established meanings of familiar words inside out and upside down has surely strayed far away from the broad high-road of human experience, in the larger and deeper sense of this word. For experience is for ever moulding and modifying the meanings of words; and the wanton misuse of them implies defiant disregard of the rulings of the "general heart" and general mind of men.

There is another feature of the empirical philosophy which is so entirely of its essence that I cannot afford to ignore it—its *anti-idealism*. The assumption that what is ultimate in analysis is ultimately real is profoundly anti-idealistic, in that it says No—a thousand times No—to the dream, the hope, the aspiration which are vital features of the inner life of the spirit; to the instinctive tendency to look for reality, for what makes life worth living, not in that which was in the beginning of things, but in "the something evermore about to be". It is true that Professor Alexander, as a typical empiric, believes in evolution; but the dead hand of Space-Time rests on all the successive levels of existence—up to "deity" itself—that "emerge" from its matrix or into which its matrix "breaks up". Each higher level owes its being to dependence on lower levels, and never really rises above them. A gain in complexity is not a gain in reality. The world was Space-Time in the beginning of things and will be Space-Time at the end. I have said this before, but need not hesitate to repeat it.

The dualism which seems to be characteristic of metaphysics as such, and is certainly characteristic of empirical metaphysics, is at open war with the idealistic leanings of man's heart.[1] Professor Alexander tells us that there are no degrees in truth, in goodness, in reality. If this is so, what is the meaning of our dream of ideal truth, of ideal good, of supreme reality? Are we content to believe that the "standardized man" is the measure of all the mind-created qualities of things? Is the apotheosis of the "divine average"

[1] A favourite dualism of Professor Alexander, and one which plays an important part in his philosophy, is that of *finite* and *infinite*. But the antithesis of finite and infinite is not really dualistic. Professor Alexander opposes the "good" infinitude of self-containedness to the "bad" infinitude of self-transcendence. Here he parts company with his fellow-"scientist", the mathematician. Astronomers tell us that the spatial universe bends back upon itself and is therefore self-contained. But they hasten to add that *because it is self-contained therefore it is finite*.

A self-contained infinite is a contradiction in terms. On its own showing (so to speak) it is incapable of self-transcendence; it is a closed system; it is imprisoned in itself. The infinite is that which eternally eludes us because it eternally transcends itself.

the highest wisdom that the empirical philosophy can attain to?

The world of sense-experience, which, for the empirical metaphysician, is the all-in-all of existence, may, for all that we know, be no more than one among many planes of being. To say that it is the only plane is a pure assumption, as dangerous, as the foundation of a system of thought, as all negative assumptions necessarily are. Professor Alexander himself admits that if there is life beyond the grave, his whole theory of things is as good as destroyed. No one in his senses believes that the external world owes its *being* to the percipient mind; but it is possible and even probable that it owes its *appearance*, in part at least, to the senses through which mind looks out upon it; it is possible that to beings with other senses than ours it might present an entirely different appearance, and might even be as imperceptible to them as are the objects of clairvoyant vision to the "standardized man".

And what is the truth about Space-Time? The most that we can affirm, even tentatively, about Space-Time in its cosmic aspect, or rather about Space *and* Time, is that Space is the theatre in which the Drama of Evolution is being played—not the Drama as a whole, for of that we know nothing, but the particular Scene of the particular Act in which we are taking part; and that the movement of the Drama, so far as it includes us, is taking place in Time, in *our* Time, in Time as we measure it.

Metaphysics has been happily defined as the attempt of a man to lift himself by his own waistband. It might also be defined as the attempt of mind (in the sense of intellect) to rise superior to its own subjectivity and attain to knowledge of objective reality. The one attempt is not more futile than the other. Wherever mind goes it takes with it its own ways of looking at things, its own weights and measures, its own tests and standards. What Professor Eddington says of the physical universe applies with even greater force to the universe as such: "The world of physics is a world contemplated from within, surveyed by appliances which are part of it and subject to its own laws. What the world might be deemed like if probed in some supernatural manner by appliances not furnished by itself we do not profess to know." But Professor Alexander does profess to know. He looks at things from the standpoint of the "angels" (his own word), and is satisfied that he sees them as they really are. "It is not the human conceptions of things", he reminds us, "which metaphysics seeks to exhibit, but the constitution of the world itself." He who can say this must have a remarkable faith in the lifting power of his own waistband. The assumption that "the constitution of the world" can be "exhibited" is in itself a human conception. And so is every other metaphysical assumption. The metaphysical treatise which is not from first to last an "exhibition" of "human conceptions of things" has not been written and will never be written. Try as we may, we have no choice but to survey the universe *from within*.

Professor Alexander, as an empirical metaphysician, identifies metaphysics with philosophy on the one hand and with science on the other. He must make his choice between metaphysics and science. He cannot both submit to the restrictions which science imposes on its votaries and enjoy the freedom to "speculate largely" which is the privilege, *de facto* if not *de jure*, of the metaphysician. Empirical metaphysics is a hybrid product of speculative thought. It is neither science nor—I was going to say metaphysics, but perhaps I had better say—philosophy. For the metaphysician claims the right to lay down the rules of the metaphysical game as he for one proposes to play it; in other words, to make assumptions at the outset which will determine the whole movement of his thought. Neither the scientist nor the philosopher makes such a claim. Each of these has a sense of responsibility which never deserts him, a loyalty from which he never swerves. The scientist works in the main in accordance with recognized rules and submits his conclusions to recognized tests. The philosopher follows the light of wisdom, as he sees it, wherever it may lead him. Let the metaphysician play his game by his own rules if it pleases him to do so, and let him flatter himself that he has won it. But let him not flatter himself that he has won the double stakes for which he played—the truth which is the reward of science, the wisdom which is the reward of philosophy.

The relation between metaphysics and philosophy may be looked at from another point of view. Take away from philosophy whatever there is in it of poetry, and whatever else may serve to differentiate it, in respect of spirit and manner, from the "bookwork" of mathematics. Take away from it its "wings" and its "song".[1] The resulting residuum may perhaps pass as metaphysics. Whether there is any *locus standi* in it for the empirical metaphysician is a matter which his fellow-metaphysicians must decide. I leave him in their hands.

[1] See the quotation from Joubert on the title-page.

CHAPTER III

# POPULAR METAPHYSICS

Let me repeat with emphasis that I mean by "metaphysics" what metaphysical experts mean by the word—namely, the *intellectual* attempt to understand the universe. That such an attempt should be made again and again is no doubt inevitable. That it should fail as often as it is made is not less inevitable. For intellect is unequal to the task which the metaphysician sets it. If it relies on itself alone and tries to arrive at ideal truth by purely logical methods, regardless of the claims of intuition and experience, it can do no more than reason deductively from its own "assumption about reality". Its conclusions will, therefore, be worth no more than its initial assumption; and that assumption will prove, when analysed, to be merely a statement of the logical laws under which intellect, when divorced from intuition and experience, is supposed to work. The logical metaphysician who flatters himself that he has solved the Supreme Problem has really done no more than lay down to his own satisfaction the rules of the metaphysical game. From these he has deduced the Universe.

Or, again, intellect can interpret the data of sense-experience by analytical methods, the results of which admit of being verified by appeals to the testimony of the senses; and it can flatter itself that what is ultimate in its analysis of sense-experience is ultimately real and therefore ideally true. But in that case the quest of ideal truth would be obviously circular, for the verification would be inconclusive except on the assumption that the data of sense-experience are intrinsically real.

But these considerations will not deter men from entering the path of metaphysical speculation. The unattainable has allurements of its own which it is hard to resist. It has been said that "man never knows how metaphysical he is"; and this saying is so far true that it holds good of the average or "standardized" man as well as of the intellectual expert. The part that the standardized man plays in metaphysical speculation is more important than we are apt to suspect. Whence do metaphysical experts get the primary assumptions which they elaborate into systems of thought? Is it not from themselves as standardized men? It is as a standardized man that the empirical metaphysician postulates the intrinsic reality of the world of sense-experience. And it is as a standardized man that the logical metaphysician defers to the authority of the Law of Contradiction and regards consistency as the proof of truth.

That being so, we must be prepared to find that there is a metaphysics of the People as well as of the Schools. The standardized man is a rough-and-ready thinker, and he works up his primary assumptions by crude but direct methods into rough-and-ready systems of thought, which he may or may not hand over to the intellectual expert for further elaboration. These systems fall for the most part under three heads: (1) *Supernaturalism*, (2) *Materialism*, (3) *Agnosticism*.

What have these philosophies to say for themselves? Supernaturalism and materialism, though violently opposed to one another, have this much in common that in them the dualistic tendency of metaphysical speculation has free play. They are therefore worth studying, if for no other reason, as being typical examples of the general trend of dualistic thought.

I have said that dualism is the Nemesis which waits on the devotion to the logic of Being, which is characteristic of a purely intellectual philosophy. At the risk of repeating myself, I must return to this theme. My excuse for doing so is that the matter is one of transcendent importance, the insidiousness of dualism—the stealth and subtlety with which it insinuates itself into our mental processes—being only equalled by its power for evil when once it has gained a footing in the mind. It is as an evil influence in philosophy that I propose to consider it; but it will be understood that when the head-waters of spirituality have been poisoned, life as a whole and character as a whole must suffer serious loss.

The logic of Being is the logic of Yes *or* No.

It presents us with alternatives and bids us choose between them. It bids us choose, for example, between *A* and *not–A*. Here there is no room for compromise. The adverb "not" is a barrier which cannot be passed. The difference between *A* and *not–A* may be minute, but the separation of the two is complete. A given stretch of road may or may not be 100 yards long. It cannot be both 100 yards long and 99 (let us say); 99 is *not* 100.

But if we are to say Yes *or* No, we must be sure that our choice lies between genuine alternatives and not between correlated opposites. I have already explained what I mean by correlated opposites. Language abounds in antithetical terms, some of which (such as *spirit* and *matter*, *reality* and *appearance*, *good* and *evil*) stand for entire aspects of Nature's being, while others (such as *pleasant* and *painful*, *high* and *low*, *strong* and *weak*) stand for no more than meridians (so to speak) of her infinite sphere. Corresponding to each pair of terms is a pair of correlated or polar opposites. I call the opposites *correlated* because, instead of being mutually exclusive, they are mutually dependent, each having its meaning by reference to the other, and losing its meaning in the event—imaginable, if not possible—of the cancellation of the other. I call them *polar* because in each case the whole movement is from pole to anti-pole, from infinity to counter-infinity, neither pole being ever met with in its ideal purity; for, though each is continuously approached, it is never actually reached. The opposite tendencies always co-exist, the one rising as the other falls and falling as the other rises, but neither being able to free itself from some admixture of the other. From one point of view they may be regarded as irreconcilable enemies; from another, as inseparable allies. For they co-operate to produce the world of our experience just as "infinity" and "nothing" co-operate to produce our finite numbers.

*To apply the Law of Contradiction to polar or correlated opposites is dualism.* There are two spheres of human activity in which dualism is rampant. Our everyday life is one sphere. Speculative philosophy is the other. In the former sphere the average man is the arch offender. He cannot well help himself. For him such and such a man is good *or* bad, clever *or* stupid, true *or* false, strong *or* weak. Or, again, the man is good or *bad*, clever or *stupid*, etc. He is not content to say that the man is good or not–good, clever or not–clever, etc. He knows well enough that every man is good *and* bad, clever *and* stupid, etc.; that the good man has his lapses from goodness, that the clever man is stupid about some things, etc. He knows well enough that there are intervening terms between polar opposites, that gradation and relativity are essential features of the world in which we live. But he cannot adequately express either gradation or relativity; and life is too short to allow of his introducing modifying clauses into all his statements. The constitution of language is dualistic, and it is hard for him to kick against the pricks. In justice to him it must be said that he does not as a rule take his own statements over-seriously. At any rate he does not lean upon them with the full weight of his conviction, except when he is excited by opposition. In the heat of argument he both overstates his case and for the moment believes in his own overstatement. That is why verbal controversy is as a rule so futile. Each of the disputants overstates his case and, with his own overstatement ringing in his ears, is deaf to the overstated arguments of the other. And the more heated the argument becomes, the wilder are the overstatements, the more vehemently are they advanced and the less impression do they make on him to whom they are addressed.

In the sphere of speculative inquiry the temptation to relapse into dualism is even stronger than in the sphere of practical everyday life. One might expect the metaphysician, with his regard for logic and consistency, to be proof against the temptation; but that would be asking too much of human nature. The metaphysician relies on intellect or pure thought for the solution of his problems; and pure thought, when it begins to speculate, must needs surround itself with abstractions. In a world of abstractions, where the modifying influence of experience and of the common sense which experience generates is wanting, where the resistance of concrete facts to the movements of thought is at its minimum, negation passes in a moment into diametrical opposition, bare existence transforms itself into the fullness of Being, non-existence transforms itself into the emptiness of non-Being, and the slightest deviation from *A* takes the mind, through an unresisting medium, to the other side (so to speak) of the universe. The confusion between negation and correlated opposition is unavoidable. The nature of things is too strong for the thinker. The pressure on him of linguistic dualism, and the refusal of the terms which he handles, words which are alive with spiritual meaning, to serve as mere counters in his game, are constraining influences which he cannot well resist.

Not that he makes much effort to resist them. As often as not he falls headlong into dualism. He deals as a rule with antithetical conceptions which range from pole to pole of existence and which, interpenetrating one another, divide the world, or at least a whole aspect of the world, between them. These he treats, as often as not, as alternatives, mutually exclusive conceptions between which we must make our final choice. This is dualism, naked and unashamed.

Bradley's treatment of "appearance and reality" is a case in point. It illustrates my meaning so aptly that I must ask leave to revert to it. "Appearance" and "reality" are antithetical conceptions which may almost be said to cover the whole range of existence, breadthwise as well as lengthwise. How does Bradley deal with them? In the earlier part of his work he treats them as alternatives. What is not "genuine reality" is "mere appearance", and nothing is genuinely real except "the Absolute". Here, then, as the direct result of deference to the logical Law of Contradiction—for it is for violating that law that the various claimants to reality have their claims disallowed—we have the illogical dualism of the Absolute, which is "genuine reality", and the phenomenal world, which is "mere appearance". In the latter part of the book Bradley tries to extricate himself from the toils of dualism by a tardy recognition of gradation in reality; and in this concession there is implicit the realization that "appearance" and "reality" are not alternatives, but correlated opposites. But the realization of this fundamental truth remains implicit. Bradley never realizes how completely his recognition of gradation in reality had changed his philosophical standpoint, or how hopeless had been the dualistic *impasse* from which it had helped him to escape.[1]

[1] But Bradley, the logical metaphysician, does recognize, however tardily, gradation in reality. The empirical metaphysician does not. His dualism is thorough and uncompromising. "There are no degrees in truth", says Professor Alexander, "and still less in reality." This sovereign dogma dominates his philosophy from end to end.

Again, it must be remembered that the metaphysician lives in an atmosphere of controversy, and that in that heated atmosphere he is as prone to overstate his case—in other words to overemphasize his dualism—as is the average man when he is dealing with the affairs of his daily life.

When popular dualism allies itself to metaphysical dualism, the former, as is usual in such cases, taking command of the situation; when popular dualism takes metaphysical dualism into its service, sets it its task, and tells it what conclusions it is expected to establish—then dualism becomes a disruptive influence which destroys the unity of the universe, giving us instead of two opposite poles—united by the process which separates them—two dissevered worlds, and instead of the infinite process itself two finite states of being, between which, in the order of nature, intercourse is impossible.

Of dualism in this extreme form there are two chief types—*supernaturalism* and *materialism*.[1] These are intimately connected, are in fact the face and the reverse of the same philosophy, both having grown out of a dualistic misinterpretation of the fundamental antithesis of *spirit* and *matter*. I need not take pains to prove that "spirit" and "matter" are correlated opposites. As far as our experience goes they always co-exist, and they

[1] It may perhaps be contended that materialism is a monistic, not a dualistic, philosophy. I will presently consider this objection.

vary together, as such opposites always do, in inverse proportion. To define either term except as the opposite of the other is, strictly speaking, impossible. There is, however, a provisional interpretation of the antithesis which throws some light on the relation of the two terms to one another—namely, that by "matter" we mean (in the last resort) what is ultimate in our analysis of the world of our experience, and by "spirit" what is ultimate in the evolutionary movement of Nature, and in the synthetic movement of our own thought. But, for popular thought, which is dominated by the logic of Yes *or* No, spirit and matter are not correlated opposites but alternatives, independent and mutually exclusive entities, which are somehow or other mysteriously conjoined. By "matter", in the crude pseudo-philosophy of the people, is meant the whole outward and visible world; and by "spirit" is meant the soul or spirit of man, which, though united with his body during his sojourn on earth, is separable from it, and will be separated from it at death.

From the dualism of Matter and Spirit there is an easy transition to the dualism of Nature and the Supernatural. "Nature" is one of the hardest-worked and worst-used words in the whole range of human speech. It has many meanings and shades of meaning; and to pin it down to any one meaning is impossible. It might perhaps be defined, loosely and provisionally, as "the way of the universe". But man early learns to distinguish between himself and the world to which he belongs, and, in doing this, to distinguish between human nature and Nature as such. In drawing this distinction he de-spiritualizes the world around him, and so prepares the ground for an interpretation of Nature, first as "the way of the material world", and then as "the material world" itself, to which he belongs as a material being, but which he rises above as a soul or spirit. In thinking of himself as rising above Nature in virtue of his spirituality, he calls into being the Supernatural world.

With this disruption of the universe into two entirely disconnected worlds, dualism takes its place, no longer as a particular feature of philosophy, but as a philosophy complete in itself, having as its counterpart a scheme of life complete in itself—in other words, a religion.

Consider what this means. The antithesis of "phenomenal" and "real" has disappeared. There are now three kinds of reality: the created reality of the material world, the created reality of the soul of man, and the creative reality of the Supernatural world. The material world is in itself what it seems to be to our perceptive faculties; but only because God, the life and soul of the Supernatural world, has made it what it is. The reality of the Supernatural world is self-existent, and therefore of a higher order than that of the material world, though in a sense it is not more real. But in effect all reality has been transferred to the world beyond Nature.[1] The reality of the material world is but an efflux from the higher world; it had a definite beginning in time, and it will return in due season to the source from which it came.

Man belongs to both worlds, and is their chief, if not their sole, bond of union. But for him they would have nothing to say to each other, and the disruption of the universe would be complete. As a material body man is a child of Nature; as a soul or spirit, a child of the Supernatural God. But he is an exile from the higher world. His dualistic philosophy demands that this should be so. The two worlds are separated by a profound abyss. If man could bestride that abyss at will it would cease to be. In order to account for his being in exile he has told himself the story of the Fall. How is he to return to his native land? If he were to remain in exile for ever, the world in which he lives would be for him the only world. He would know of no other. And if he continued to know of no other, he would be no better than the beasts that perish. The world in which he lives can do nothing for him. Its reality is mere actuality. The Supernatural world is the real world. If he is to receive the guiding light which he calls *wisdom* and the sustaining strength which he calls

[1] From which, however, it will drain away into the abyss which separates the two worlds.

*grace*, these must come to him from the other side of the impassable abyss. Impassable from his side. The Supernatural God can of course pass it at will. But because He is supernatural, the intercourse which He holds with man is not normal and necessary, but arbitrary and miraculous. The abyss remains unbridged. There are no pipe-lines crossing it for the transmission of wisdom and grace. Or if there are, their taps are kept under supernatural control. If man could help himself at will to those life-giving waters he would have returned from exile. The word "supernatural" would have lost its meaning. "What is universal is natural." If wisdom and grace were as much at man's service as are sunshine and air, the distinction between the two worlds would be cancelled and Nature would be all in all.

In the interest of his dualistic philosophy man must think of God as using special channels for His self-revelation, special channels for His beneficent activity. He must have His chosen prophets, His chosen ministers, His chosen churches or church. But how is man to test the credentials of those who claim to be the accredited messengers of God? There is no answer to this question. Belief in a supernatural revelation is the special gift of the Supernatural God. So the theology of the Supernatural admits, or rather insists. This is a fatalistic begging of the question. But that cannot be helped. The "assumption about reality", which is implicit in the dualism of Nature and the Supernatural, controls the philosophy of the Supernatural in all its developments, formulates the Laws of Thought by reference to which its own authenticity is to be tested, and ends by proving itself to its own satisfaction. The dualistic logic of the people is reinforced by the dualistic logic of the Schools, receiving from the latter as formal authorization what it has given to it as secret support. From philosophy to theology, from theology to ethics, from ethics to conduct, the current of dualistic thought runs its course without let or hindrance. The choice between the "mighty opposites", which is metaphysical on one level, becomes emotional on a second, instinctive on a third, practical on a fourth. Reason, imagination, sentiment, conscience—all play their parts in the great drama. The choice between the Supernatural and Nature becomes a choice between God and the Devil, between good and evil, between salvation and perdition, between Heaven and Hell.

These are general statements. They can easily be illustrated by examples. The Church of Rome is the arch-champion of dualism in general and supernaturalism in particular. Its philosophy, which is essentially metaphysical, its doctrine, its policy and its practice are all dualistic through and through. And its dualism is so thoroughgoing that it is ever tending to degenerate into separatism. The God whom it worships separates Himself "really and in essence" from the world as such. The Church, believing itself to be the sole intermediary between God and man, separates itself from all other churches and virtually excommunicates the rest of mankind. Also, as a spiritual institution, it separates itself from the whole secular world. The priesthood separates itself from the laity. The Pope separates himself from the rest of the priesthood. The religious life separates itself from the secular life. Religious education separates itself from secular education. Orthodoxy separates itself from heresy. Faith from infidelity. Grace from "nature". Heroic virtue from ordinary virtue. Venial sin from mortal sin. The children of grace separate themselves from the children of wrath. The sanctified from the reprobate. The saved from the lost. Even in the outward world there are similar and equally deep cleavages. Consecrated buildings separate themselves from all other buildings. Consecrated ground from all other ground. The consecrated elements from all other material things. And so on; for this list might be indefinitely extended.

And there is a constant tendency, as we know from experience, for separatism, so far as it affects the social life of man, to degenerate into aloofness, contempt, aversion, intolerance, fanaticism, self-exaltation, anger, hatred, strife. When opposites, which are mutually dependent, which owe to one another their respective meanings, their respective titles to existence, and which ought to co-operate with one another in and through their reciprocal opposition, are forcibly disjoined by metaphysical dualism, what can they do but glare angrily at one another across the abyss which separates them? Each of them has missed its destiny through being separated from the other, and each blames the other for the tragedy in which both are involved. But the real causes of the tragedy are man's inability to present to his consciousness the deeper workings of his heart and mind, and his naïve assumption that this mental limitation determines, not relatively but absolutely, the "Laws of Thought".

We see, then, that when metaphysical dualism, popular dualism and practical dualism reinforce one another and play into one another's hands, we get an explosive of almost annihilative force. The disruption of the universe become all-pervasive. Great gaps open up in all directions, which cannot by any natural agency be fathomed or spanned. On every plane of being, in every department of life, polar opposites present themselves as alternatives between which we must make our choice. Mutual exclusion takes the place of correlated opposition; conflict, of co-operation; oscillation between Yes and No, of gradation and relativity; self-consistency, of self-transcendence; dogmatism, whether positive or negative, of the free movement of open-minded thought.

And this is not all. In the world as a whole and in each of its aspects and departments, wherever a gap opens up between opposites it drains into itself first the infinitude and then the reality of the principles or tendencies or worlds which it divides. Let us consider the dualism of the Heaven and Hell of orthodox theology. "There are probably as many degrees—(may I be allowed to repeat my own words?)—of moral worth as there have been men since the world began; and in regard to their temptations and opportunities no two men are or have been exactly alike. Yet in the requital of moral worth we recognize no middle term between two diametrically opposite and infinitely dissevered extremes. And those extremes are states, not processes. To enter Heaven is to be saved. To enter Hell is to be lost. Thereafter nothing matters. But the difference between Heaven and Hell, the difference between infinite and everlasting happiness and infinite and everlasting misery, is unfathomable by any plummet of imagination or thought. By comparison with it all differences within the limits of Heaven or Hell —the difference between the happiness of the soul which has just escaped Hell and the happiness of the highest archangel, the difference between the misery of the soul which has just missed Heaven and the misery (if he is miserable) of the Prince of Darkness—are as nothing. So long as we think of Heaven and Hell as states, so long as we invest them with finality, all our efforts to raise to infinity the glory of the one state and the gloom of the other are vain. The gulf which divides them drains into itself the infinitude of both the worlds, both the states of being which it divides."[1]

This example is typical of what happens when a process which ranges from pole to anti-pole is broken up by dualistic thought into two states of being, parted by an impassable gulf. And with infinitude goes reality. For the ideal is the real, and infinitude is of the very essence of the quest of the ideal. The draining away of reality takes various forms. In the case of Nature and the Supernatural the intervening gulf drains into itself *spirituality* from the side of Nature and *actuality* from the side of the Supernatural, leaving a dead world on one side of it and a world of shadows on the other. For dualism deprives each of two correlated opposites of the very element of reality which it owes to the other.

So much for the effect of metaphysical dualism on the philosophy of the Supernatural. Its effect on institutional policy and personal character and conduct will be equally disastrous. The Church which believes itself to be divinely commissioned, to be the sole depository of revealed truth, the

[1] *The Secret of the Cross.*

sole agency for the distribution of supernatural grace, the sole custodian of the Keys of Heaven, will be dogmatic as a teacher, tyrannical as a ruler, separatist in its attitude towards the rest of mankind; intolerant of dissentient opinion; the implacable enemy of freedom in thought and action; ruthless in its choice of weapons; ready to sell salvation for submission, for deference, for blind obedience, for material support; making its appeal to base motives, to selfish fears, to ignoble hopes, to spiritual indolence, to the desire to buy salvation in the cheapest market, i.e. at the least expenditure of spiritual effort. If just to escape perdition is to achieve salvation, it stands to reason that the minimum of attainment is all that can be demanded from the believer, and that the desire to attain to the prescribed minimum, to pass a qualifying test, will too often take the place of the devotion to an unattainable ideal, which is the mainspring and should be the master motive of man's spiritual life.

The loss of infinitude which is characteristic of metaphysical dualism, the disappearance of the infinite from each of the dissevered worlds into the abysmal depths of the intervening void, reproduces itself in practical life—in the life of the community or institution, in the life of the individual—as loss of idealism, as loss of spirituality, as the materialization of motives, as the mechanization of life.

But the failure of Supernaturalism as a scheme of life is not accompanied by any sense of self-distrust on the part of its metaphysical exponents. Belief in its own infallibility is indeed of the very essence of supernaturalism. The metaphysician, moving at will through the world of abstractions with which he has surrounded himself, carried away by his own trains of thought, convinced by his own arguments, is tempted to make general statements about the world of concrete realities in which he lives, which are not only unsupported by experience, but are sometimes at open variance with it. In supernaturalism belief in revelation greatly facilitates this *a priori* construction of the world. By reasoning deductively from premises which are supposed to have been supernaturally communicated to man, metaphysical ingenuity is able to construct, with some approach to precision, a quasi-science of first principles and fundamental facts, in which cosmology, anthropology and theology become one. The official creeds, for example, and the religious manuals of Christendom make authoritative statements about the greatest of all great matters, about man and God, about earth and heaven, about this life and the next, with an assurance which is made possible by the fact that the statements cannot be proved by an appeal to experience, and cannot, however repugnant they may be to right reason and common sense, be formally disproved.

And the pity of it is that, when logic is divorced from experience and intuition, if one's premises are unsound in any respect or degree, the more correct the procedure the more erroneous will be the conclusions; for in the atmosphere of the syllogism the taint of unsoundness spreads with fatal facility, so that what goes into a syllogistic process as a plausible assumption may well come out of it as an outrage on right reason and common sense. More especially is this the case when philosophical problems are being discussed; for then the instability of the terms that are used, their readiness to change their meaning from context to context and from mind to mind, makes reliance on deduction a fruitful source of error, confusion of thought and self-deception. And however repugnant a conclusion may be to right reason and common sense, whatever defects one's intuitive judgment may find in it, the fact that it has been correctly deduced from accepted premises is held to give it immunity from adverse criticism. Hence it is, to take pertinent examples, that the sale of Indulgences has been defended by responsible theologians as a practical deduction from a theoretically defensible doctrine—that of the "Treasury of the Church"; and that in the doctrine of Papal Infallibility we have the *reductio ad absurdum* of a group of associated assumptions —about God and man, about God and Christ, about Christ and the Church—from which the doctrine claims, with some show of reason, to have been logically deduced.

Supernaturalism has done its work and had its day. There was work for it to do in a certain stage in human progress. It did that work, but it is now outstaying its welcome. It raised the level of man's life, though at a heavy cost, for legalism, ceremonialism, superstition and priestcraft have ever been its satellites. The idea of evolution is now undermining its metaphysical foundation and discrediting the dualism which has been its temporary strength, but also its abiding weakness. There was a time when it was in itself the main current of belief and thought. To-day it has the option of transforming itself into harmony with what is now the main current, or, by continuing to resist the idea of evolution, of becoming a side current which will lose itself sooner or later in stagnant pools and sandy wastes. If it is to transform itself, it must abandon the worn-out metaphysics which has made it mistake words for things and rules of logic for laws of Nature, and adopt a saner, a more realistic and a more spiritual philosophy.

A reaction against Supernaturalism gives us Materialism. The dualism of Nature and the Supernatural has grown out of the dualism of Matter and Spirit; and the boundaries of Nature and the Supernatural correspond roughly, in popular thought, with the boundaries of the worlds of Matter and Spirit. Denial of the Supernatural will therefore readily transform itself into denial of the reality of Spirit. When this happens we get Materialism as a philosophy and a creed.

Materialism, as a philosophy, is the product of many factors, all closely interrelated. Among these may be mentioned:—

The current confusion, dualistic in character, between the *actual* and the *real*; the cognate confusion, also dualistic, between the *supernormal* and the *supernatural*; the undue reliance on intellect which the achievements of physical science tend to foster; the consequent assumption that quantitative analysis is the road to reality; the further assumption that phenomena which are or seem to be unamenable to a purely intellectual treatment are non-existent, and that stories of their occurrence must be rejected on *a priori* grounds; and the implicit assumption that aspects of the universe, such as the (so-called) spiritual world, which, when we try to interpret them, take intellect out of its depths, are phantasmal, worlds of shadows and dreams.

The materialist is not always content to give his philosophy the name which properly belongs to it. Sometimes he speaks of it as Naturalism, sometimes as Realism. The disinterested student of philosophy cannot but protest against the wanton limitation of the idea of Nature which is involved in the use of the former word, and the question-begging assumption about Reality which is involved in the use of the latter.

The materialist contends that the outward and visible world is the whole world, and that it is in itself what it seems to be to our perceptive faculties. This is materialism in its crude or popular form. There are refinements of materialism which do not go so far as this; but they all go so far as to say that the outward and visible world is intrinsically real, and some of them pass on from this to the assumption that analysis is the road to reality, and that what is ultimate in our analysis of "matter" is ultimately real. There is this to be said for Supernaturalism, whatever may be its defects as a system of thought, that in it man reminds himself that the spiritual pole of existence is the positive or real pole. Materialism transfers reality to the anti-pole. In doing so it accepts by implication the idea of gradation in reality, an idea which is, strictly speaking, foreign to it; but occasional lapses into inconsistency must be allowed to the materialist as to metaphysicians of other schools.

Why do I speak of materialism as dualistic? The materialist calls himself a monist, and his contention that the material world is the whole world seems at first sight to justify his claim to that title. But if we look into the matter more closely we shall have to disallow his claim. For he agrees with the supernaturalist in dividing the universe into two worlds, and his denial of reality to one of those worlds does not alter the dualistic character of his initial assumption. He does not restore wholeness to the universe by mutilating it. The gulf which separates the material from the spiritual world remains. The material world is not enlarged in the slightest degree by his denial of reality to the spiritual world. Its infinitude disappeared into the gulf which divided the two worlds, before he began to examine their respective claims to reality; and he cannot recover it. What the gulf now does is to divide actuality from illusion. Reality, which has its counterpart in infinitude, continues to elude the grasp of his thought.

In what respect does popular materialism differ from the "empirical philosophy", the exposition of which in Professor Alexander's *Time, Space and Deity* I have recently studied? In no essential respect, as far as I can see, except that it is openly and avowedly materialistic. Professor Alexander indignantly denies that he is a materialist. Yet he regards the world of sense-experience as intrinsically and exclusively real, and believes that by analysing the data of sense-experience "to the death" he can arrive at fundamental reality. Why he should disclaim the title of materialist I cannot see. He virtually identifies the mind with the brain—psychoses with neuroses

—and he rules out the possibility of the soul outliving the body. It is true that physical science, with which the New Realism (as it calls itself) is closely allied, has recently carried its analysis of matter so far as, in a sense, to dematerialize it, resolving it into "a schedule of pointer-values", and the material world into "a complex of metrical symbols". But the dematerialization of matter, if accepted by the materialist, does not make his philosophy the less materialistic; for it is not the ascription of reality to dense matter, as such, that is of the essence of materialism, but the assumption that through the scientific analysis of dense matter lies the road to ultimate reality. Empirical metaphysics, as expounded by Professor Alexander, seems to me to share with the older and cruder forms of materialism the fatalistic, in the last resort the mechanistic, conception of life which is characteristic of the latter. And, as the reputed headquarters of reality, the Space-Time of the empirical metaphysician does not materially differ from the atoms of Epicurus and his predecessors or from the outward world (as real as it seems to be) of the materialistically minded average man.

Of the ethical implications of materialism, of its general influence on character and conduct, I need not speak at length. That in individual cases the conscious acceptance of a materialistic creed can co-exist with a high sense of duty and a life of active virtue, is indisputable; and in such cases the very pessimism and anti-idealism of the adopted creed may well raise the life of virtue to a high level of heroism. But that the general tendency of materialism, as a system of thought, and therefore as a scheme of life, is to ally itself with the selfishness and individualism of the natural man, and so demoralize character and conduct, can scarcely be doubted. There is something in each of us of the man who says in his heart, "Let us eat and drink, for to-morrow we die"; and there is something of the man who says to himself, "The palpable is the real, and I know of no other test of reality". And when one's theoretical materialism, being consciously realized and accepted, gives formal support to one's practical materialism, the restraints which conventional religion and morality impose on the latter will be seriously weakened, if not wholly removed.

The materialist sometimes calls himself an agnostic; but as a rule he is quite as dogmatic, even while he is professing agnosticism, as any official exponent of supernaturalism. In materialism, as in other metaphysical systems of thought, the transition from speculative conviction to dogmatic assertion is easily made. But in materialism the dogmatic statements are as a rule negative rather than positive. Limits are imposed on the universe—limits which man's normal experience prescribes—which it is not allowed to pass. The supernormal is confounded with the supernatural, and is ruled out as illusory and impossible. The terms in which man expresses his instinctive belief in the reality of spiritual things are regarded as a delusive shorthand which the materialist uses so as to avoid the tiresome circumlocutions which he would otherwise have to resort to. But his use of them does not shake his conviction that they have no real content. He is careful to remind us, for example, that when the brain ceases to function "the soul" ceases to exist.[1] Stories of other worlds, other lives, other planes of being, are dismissed on *a priori* grounds as the products of imagination, or hallucination, or fraud.

Of all forms of philosophical dogmatism that of the materialist is the least defensible. Negative statements are proverbially hard to prove. The evidence for the reality and supremacy of spirit—the revelation of self to self—cannot be weighed by reason, and is therefore impervious to criticism and *a fortiori* to disproof. The evidence for the supernormal accumulates from day to day, and is to-day overwhelmingly strong. But no amount of unwelcome evidence can shake the faith—or unfaith—which is securely rooted in metaphysical prejudice.

[1] As Sir Arthur Keith has recently done. Sir Arthur is a distinguished scientist. When he made that dogmatic assertion he had unwittingly relapsed into metaphysics.

The materialist's philosophy has of course a positive as well as a negative side, and on the former he is quite as dogmatic as on the latter. His dualistic identification of existence with reality leads him to assume that intrinsic reality, reality as it is in itself, can be known by man—consciously known, scientifically known, known *about*, known as the properties of a triangle or the parts of a flower are known. This assumption separates man from the world which surrounds him, separates reality from experience, and enables man to contemplate the world critically, impersonally, unemotionally, *from without*. Contemplating it from that standpoint the materialist analyses it into what seem to be its ultimate elements, and says of them, "these are self-contained, self-centred, self-existent, *real*". He does not realize that in pronouncing this judgment he has postulated the existence of a second centre of reality—*his own mind*.

A reaction against materialism—a sentimental reaction against its pessimism, an intellectual reaction against its dogmatism—has led many metaphysically minded thinkers to take refuge in agnosticism. The word "agnosticism" is used in many senses and has a wide range of meaning. There is an agnosticism, for example, which has its counterpart in a profound and vivid faith—a faith so profound that it has no need of mental satisfaction, and so vivid, so truly alive, that it regards imprisonment in words as an outrage. But for such an agnosticism to be possible the mind must have freed itself from reliance on intellect for the solution of ultimate problems; in other words, from bondage to metaphysics. Agnosticism, as the word is ordinarily used, means nothing less than the final failure of the whole metaphysical adventure. The agnostic's faith in the capacity of intellect is unbounded; so much so, indeed, that he instinctively takes for granted that what intellect cannot know cannot be known. The agnostic attitude, the abandonment of the whole field of philosophical speculation, is therefore an admission by a whole-hearted intellectualist that intellect cannot, in any respect or degree, understand the universe—an admission, by one who has tried to think metaphysically, of the inherent futility of metaphysics.

## CHAPTER IV

# INTUITIONAL PHILOSOPHY

*The Claims of Feeling.*—I shall perhaps be reminded that so far I have not mentioned the word "idealism". Is not Idealism a branch or school or aspect of philosophy? Of philosophy—yes. Of metaphysics—I am not so sure. The philosophy of the Absolute claims to be idealistic. And perhaps one may say that in it Idealism makes its nearest approach to the status of a metaphysical system. But it is not a very near approach. So far as the philosophy of the Absolute is idealistic it is not strictly metaphysical. In order to bring the Absolute within the compass of human experience and so make it the object of idealistic aspiration and endeavour, it finds it necessary to call "feeling" and "volition" to the aid of "thought", thereby confessing that the latter is unequal to the task of "knowing reality". And when, in response to the demands of spiritual "common sense", it accepts the idealistic conception of gradation in reality, it throws the Law of Contradiction to the winds, and with it the formal logic to which it owes allegiance. In thus departing from the path of metaphysical rectitude it commits the crime, unpardonable from its own point of view, of contradicting itself.

The truth is that idealism has never been, and

can never be, strictly metaphysical. Its central assumption, that of the reality and supremacy of Spirit, it owes not to any process of reasoning or even of intellectual meditation, but to direct introspection. The spirit of man reveals itself to itself, and in doing so shines by no other light than its own. Its self-revelation cannot justify itself to reason and has no need to do so. In the philosophy of the Upanishads, in which, as it seems to me, idealism touches its high-water mark, there is more of poetry than of metaphysics. The sages of Ancient India seem to have reached their daringly defiant, their sublimely paradoxical conclusions, not by thinking out the great problems that confronted them, but by feeling their way—by living their way, one might almost say—into the very heart of them.

What differentiates idealism from other philosophies is that in it feeling insists on immingling itself with thought and becoming the senior partner in the business of thinking. Is it justified in doing so? I will try to answer this question.

Metaphysics identifies itself with philosophy. Philosophy is "love of wisdom". Wisdom is the guiding light irradiated from the central core of Reality. Therefore the true, the final aim of philosophy is *to know reality*, to know it so well as to be able to distinguish it, in its various degrees, from imposture and illusion. This is the avowed aim of the metaphysician. But he assumes that to know reality is to know *about* reality as one knows about this or that object of material experience and scientific investigation. He assumes that one can detach oneself from reality, set it apart from oneself, contemplate it from without, study it coldly, critically, analytically, ascertain its properties, formulate its laws, map out its contents, and present the knowledge of it which has been thus acquired to one's consciousness for acceptance or rejection. He assumes, in other words, that intellect, pure and simple, is competent to "understand the universe", to "know reality".

This assumption involves a further assumption as to the constitution of the universe and the nature of reality, which amounts to a potential begging of the whole question. For intellect is most at home and does its best work when it is dealing either with lifeless abstractions or with material things. And to assume that it is competent to solve the greatest of all problems is (by implication) to degrade "that which is ultimate and uttermost" to the level of a lifeless abstraction or a material thing.

"Knowledge of reality." How is this to be gained? *Reality*, as a philosophical concept, has a wider range than *life*, which it underlies and embraces and transcends. How is knowledge of life to be gained? Not by speculating about life. Not by reasoning about it. Not by trying to comprehend it. Not by entrusting to intellect the task of exploring and reporting on it.[1] *But by trying to live it.* By trying to realize its possibilities, to fathom its depths, to follow out its tendencies, to respond to its stimuli, to open the lock-gates of our being to its inrushing flood.

Is it not the same with knowledge of reality? If we are to *know* reality, in the ultimate sense of the word, we must try to widen and deepen our experience of reality; we must try to explore, more widely and more intimately, the world in which we live, the world which centres in self, and which self claims as its own; we must try to pass beyond the horizon of conscious selfhood into the larger world that envelops it; we must try to outgrow self, to transcend self, to awake the dormant powers, undreamed of or (at best) faintly guessed at, which will bring us into touch with that larger world and unveil its realities to us; we must try, in fine, *to live our way into the heart of Reality.* To get outside Reality, to survey it from without, to map it out, to delimit its frontiers, to catalogue its contents, to enumerate its attributes, is the idlest of dreams.

If we are to know Reality we must be content to know it from within, following it out in this or that direction till its infinitude rises up like a wall of darkness and forbids our further advance.

[1] These things may be done. They have their value. But they cannot give us the intimate, illuminating knowledge that we need.

What we can know from without, what we can see, feel, handle, weigh, measure, analyse, describe in detail, talk about, think about, is relatively unreal. The Knower, who can do these things, is of a higher order of reality than the objects of his knowledge. For that very reason he cannot know himself as he knows the things that lie around him. His depths are unfathomed. His possibilities are unrealized. If he would know self—the higher self, the real self, the Self which is beyond all selves—he must try to fathom his own depths, to realize his own possibilities, in obedience to the law of growth, which is the master law of life.

In metaphysics man elaborates his own intellectual limitations into an instrument for the research of ultimate truth. These limitations centre in his inability to present to his own consciousness the deeper workings of his spirit. The larger aspects and more vital issues of life are the objects of direct perception rather than of logical and quasi-scientific analysis, and cannot be contemplated without profound emotion. It follows that, if we are to think about great matters, our thought must be in large measure intuitional and emotional. In its attempt to apprehend such matters, thought mingles itself more or less closely with feeling, to which it gives as coherence and concentration what it receives back from it as subtlety, as vision, as the power of winding itself more or less closely into the heart of things. To disentangle thought from the higher developments of feeling is impossible. So far as the attempt is made, it is accompanied, step for step, by the withdrawal of reality from the objects of our thinking, the result being that pure thought wanders at will through a world of lifeless and half-meaningless abstractions, inebriated by the exuberance of its own pseudo-scientific verbosity, deluded by specious but hollow arguments, mistaking correctness of logical procedure for conclusiveness in demonstration, and seeking premature repose—for it set out in a spirit of high adventure—in unverified and unverifiable theories.

This is harmless enough so long as the thinker realizes that he is playing a game, pitting his intellect against that of some fellow-player, and happy if he can score points more freely than his adversary. But the temptation to take himself seriously is, as we have seen, too strong for the metaphysician. So seriously does he take himself that we find him at last explaining to the universe, in general and even in detail, how it is constituted and how it is expected to behave. We find Bradley, for example, deciding, on *a priori* grounds, that "souls do not influence each other except through their bodies", in defiance of the fact, no longer disputable, that telepathy is a phenomenon of comparatively frequent occurrence. Reliance on pure thought, without regard to experience or to the feeling which experience generates, for the solution of the supreme problem, leads at last to the *a priori* construction of the world in which we live. Surrounded as he is by the creations of his own mind, the metaphysician is sure, sooner or later, to mistake these phantasms for concrete realities. We smile when he pats the universe on the back, assuring it, among other things, that it is "perfect in all its details" and "equally true and good throughout". But when once the thinker has turned his back on experience, there is nothing to check the flight of his unemotional and hyperlogical imagination into the shadow-world, void and unresisting as empty space, which it creates for itself as it passes through it. The sense of humour, which puts the brake on reason when it begins to run away with the reasoner, dies in the unoxygenated atmosphere of abstract thought; and when it is dead the mind has lost the power of criticizing itself.

We have seen that when Bradley had concentrated reality in the Absolute, he realized, too late, that for apprehension of the Absolute, "mere thought", being essentially "relational and discursive", was helpless without the co-operation of "feeling" and "will". He realized, in other words, that for knowledge of reality was needed, not thought alone, but a "higher unity", in which thought *is* "entangled with other functions of our being". As the aim of metaphysical speculation is to know reality, it follows from this concession on the part of a typical metaphysician, that the true instrument for the research of ultimate truth is the "higher unity" in which feeling and will take their places by the side of thought, losing themselves in it and absorbing it into themselves. If this inference is accepted—and I do not see how it can be avoided—the whole metaphysical structure, which is, on the metaphysician's own showing, the creation of dis-"entangled" thought, collapses like a house built of cards.

But having used feeling and will, especially the former, to buttress thought when the inadequacy of thought could no longer be ignored, Bradley threw them over without hesitation when it suited his purpose to do so. Or rather he threw feeling over; will he seems to have tacitly ignored. When he arrived at the conception—suicidal from his own point of view—of gradation in reality, he had to ask himself by what standard gradation in reality was to be measured. He saw that the problem was one for feeling to deal with as well as for thought; but he now chose to assume, in oblivion or in defiance of his own conception of the "higher unity", that his choice lay between "mere feeling" and pure thought, and that if "mere feeling" was unequal to the task of solving one of the greatest of all philosophical problems, the task must be entrusted to pure thought. Thus when "feeling" had served his purpose, he was able, by a perverse relapse into dualism, to discharge it from his service, and to entrust to "thought", disentangled once more "from other functions of our being", the task—the duty and the privilege—of interpreting the universe.

Our choice does not lie between mere feeling and pure thought. The great literatures of the world, which contain its best philosophy, and which no thinker, not even the most fanatical of metaphysicians, can afford to ignore, are the product, not of pure thought nor of mere feeling, but of thought co-operating with feeling; of thought transfigured and subtilized by feeling, and of feeling concentrated and disciplined by thought. Our choice lies between reliance on thought alone and reliance on that blend of thought and feeling by which the great critics of life, whatever may be their several mediums of expression, have established and maintained intercourse with the great realities that challenged their minds and inspired their hearts. In other words, our choice lies between logic and experience, between the formulated logic of Being and the unformulated, the secret, subtle, unselfconscious logic of Becoming, through which experience moulds us, with or without our co-operation, to its will.

We live our lives in the world of Becoming. We are subjected to the inexorable pressure of its many-sided movement on every plane of our being, at every moment in our lives, in every nerve and muscle of our bodies, in every fibre of our souls. Our response to that pressure is *feeling*. The range of feeling is as wide as that of the environing world. Its depths are unfathomable. Its possibilities are unlimited. It is in order that we may adjust ourselves well and wisely, through the medium of trained and enlightened feeling, to the world of Becoming, that we seek for the knowledge of reality which will give us the guiding light of wisdom. How can we leave feeling out when we try to gain that knowledge? The degree of reality in any object of experience is to be measured, not by the conformity of the object to the demands of a formula, but by the quality of the feeling which it awakes in our hearts. If, then, we would know reality we must take feeling into partnership with thought, each supplementing the other and, in doing so, transforming it into its own higher self; feeling which has been disciplined by thought, being as much more *sensitive* than "mere feeling", as thought which has been magnetized by feeling is more *intelligent* than "mere thought".

Such a fusion of thought and feeling is what we call *intuition*. It is in the school of experience that intuition is evolved and trained.

*The Poetic Quest of Wisdom.*—"Experience teaches." This is an old and faithful saying; and there is no aspect of life, no sphere of activity, no plane of being, to which it fails to apply. How does experience teach? By punishing us for our errors, whether wilful or blind. By making us suffer when we stray from the right path or fail to find it. By rewarding us when we find the right path and keep to it. In fine, by making us realize that the way of conformity to the truth of things is the way of well-being and happiness, and that "the way of the transgressors", even of the involuntary transgressors, "is hard".

Experience does this for us, and this counts for much in our lives. And in doing this it does more than this. It enables us to realize our infinite potentialities. Each of us has a general capacity for evolving special capacities, special senses, special faculties of direct perception, of intuitive apprehension, in response to the demands of special environments. Experience provides us with the environments that we need and teaches us through its system of rewards and punishments to adapt ourselves to them and to evolve the corresponding senses. The most precious of its rewards is the increased power that it gives us of finding the right path and walking in it. And the severest of its punishments is the increased difficulty of returning to the right path that is involved in each departure from it.

That man has a general capacity for evolving special senses cannot be doubted. In every calling, in every art, in every craft, in every recreation, in every sport or game, we make progress by gradually evolving a special sense which gives us intuitive and largely subconscious knowledge of the laws and properties of our subject-matter, knowledge which expresses itself in and is itself enlarged and deepened by appropriate action, the special sense being in each case continuously developed and strengthened by the use that we make of it, "made perfect", as the saying goes, "by practice".

There is no sphere of human activity in which this general law fails to operate. In art, in science, in literature, in scholarship, in research, in education, in social life, in politics, in war, in commerce, in finance, in manufacturing industry, in the practice of law, medicine, surgery, engineering, and other learned professions, experience enables us to evolve the senses and sub-senses that will make it possible for us to deal successfully with the matter in which we are interested.

When the intuitive faculty is working on a high level and on a large scale; when its vision is so penetrative and so apocalyptic that no medium of expression but that of poetry or creative art will content it—we call it *genius*; and we talk about "inspiration", "the fine phrenzy", "the divine madness" and the like. But even at its highest level, even when it is most genuinely inspired, the art in which genius expresses itself is still working within the limits, the illimitable limits, of experience; it is still *mimetic* (in Aristotle's sense of the word), still imitative of reality, still a record of what has been seen and felt. It is true that the reality is hidden, impalpable, unapparent to myopic, or superficial, or careless or untrained vision. But it is there—it has always been there—an essential element in the world that surrounds us, a "master presence", waiting to be discovered, waiting to be revealed. To imitate what is palpable is to copy. To imitate what is hidden is to create.

Will our capacity for evolving senses or intuitive faculties in response to the pressure and stimulus of experience ever fail us? I do not see why it should. The empirical world is our only world; but it is enough and more than enough for us, for its limits are eternally recessive. Experience can never be transcended except from within itself. If the transcendental world were a real world, separated, like the supernatural world of orthodox theology, from the world of our experience by an abyss which was impassable except from the farther side, we should have no means of apprehending it or even of knowing whether it did or did not exist. And if it revealed itself to us, or rather if someone, speaking in its name, undertook to reveal it to us, we should have no means of verifying his statements, no means of telling whether the revelation of which he claimed to have been the recipient was a reality or a fraud.

So long as the transcendental world is regarded as distinct "really and in essence" from the empirical world, the dream of exploring it, whether by metaphysical speculation or by guidance from within itself, is of all dreams the vainest. What is beyond the reach of experience, which is at once the basis of our guesses at truth and the only means of verifying them, is neither existent nor non-existent. The category of Being does not apply to it. It is as unsubstantial as a forgotten dream.

But if the dualism of "empirical" and "transcendental" is to be transcended, we must not content ourselves, as the materialist does, with the mere denial of the latter; *we must absorb the transcendental world into the empirical.* We must find room, within the ever-receding limits of experience, not only for the intangible, the immaterial and the inexplicable, but also for the incredible and the seemingly impossible. Normality is a boundary line which we have drawn for our own convenience. We must be ready to pass beyond it. We must pass beyond Aristotle's saying that "what seems to all men . . . is". The existence of clairvoyant faculties cannot be denied; and though these may be latent in all men, they are awake and active in very few. But the day is coming when they will have to be seriously reckoned with; their claims to authenticity scientifically investigated; their data weighed and measured and used as a base for fresh adventures into the unknown.

And whatever revelations our clairvoyant senses may make to us, whatever experiences they may have in store for us, we may be sure of one thing. They will be experiences. They will enlarge, widen, perhaps deepen, perhaps sublimate the world of our experience. They will not take us beyond its limits, for it has no limits. There may be no place for the supernormal in a merely intellectual philosophy; for intellect is ill at ease when "nature" begins to overflow the banks within which our thought has confined it. But the intuitional philosophy, which is content to explore the wonder-world of experience, can assimilate all supernormal happenings, and can even welcome them as widening the horizon and so stimulating the vision of the "seer".

Clairvoyant faculties are, as I have said, awake and active in few of us. That they admit of being evolved and trained by self-discipline of various kinds is possible; but that is a question which we need not pause to consider. For there is no one, whether "psychically" gifted or not, who cannot if he will evolve an intuitional philosophy of his own. If one cannot evolve it, in the goodly company of the poets, the prophets and the mystics, on the plane of spiritual emotion, one can at least evolve it on the plane of conduct, of practical moral life.

A man's intuitional philosophy is the outcome and tentative expression of his deepest convictions about the deeper realities and the larger issues of life. Experience in such matters—experience, much of which he will have to gain for himself, if he is to escape from the beaten tracks of life and so free himself from the tyranny of custom and convention—will generate sooner or later appropriate senses. It will give him insight into the laws and properties of the higher planes of being, of Nature as a living whole, of human nature in the pageant of its evolution, of the inward and spiritual life, of the mysterious world of Self. It will give him in fine a vision of reality, for which he must needs find, or try to find, fitting and adequate expression.

His attempts to express himself will take various forms. There is one medium of expression which is open to all men—conduct. Of this I will presently speak. But I am now thinking of the man who is, more or less consciously, a "lover of wisdom", a seeker for guiding light, an explorer of hidden reality. Let us assume that his experiences transcend those of ordinary men; that his vision has a wider sweep; that it goes deeper into the heart of things. How is he to tell us what he has seen and felt?

Here temperament and other constituent elements of idiosyncrasy assert themselves and determine the medium through which his vision of reality is to express itself. Creative art is one such medium. Poetry is another. But the word poetry has two meanings. Sometimes it covers the whole range of inspired literature and the whole range of creative art. Sometimes it means no more than a particular craft, the craft of the versifier, the craft which provides for the expression of emotion through the medium of rhythmical speech, of "words in tuneful order stored". I propose in this chapter to use the word in its larger sense.

In the sphere of philosophy the real rival to metaphysics, which is a quasi-scientific effort of the mind, is *poetry*. Of poetry, in the larger sense of the word, there are three chief exponents, the *artist*, the *prophet*, and the *mystic*. Will the artist give us what the metaphysician offers but cannot give—ideal truth? The great artist, whether his medium of expression be painting, sculpture, architecture, words or music, is one in whom the vision of reality awakes admiration, rising at its highest level to love, and to whom therefore reality reveals itself as *beauty*. His work in life is to pass on that revelation, to appeal to the heart by unveiling to it the beauty which is a vital aspect of reality. With truth for its own sake he has no direct concern. By truth, if he uses the word, he means artistic sincerity, fidelity to his vision.

He is no philosopher, except so far as we are all philosophers in the secret recesses of our souls. He does not offer us the guiding light which we call *wisdom*, and the desire for which is the mainspring of philosophic effort. He can give us refreshment, stimulus, inspiration. He does not pretend to give us wisdom.[1]

For this we must turn to the prophet and the mystic. Each of these has sought for reality where it dwells most fully and hides itself most securely—in the heart of man. The prophet seeks for reality in "the general heart of men"; the mystic in his own heart.

The prophet looks out on the world of human life as it surges around him and as it unfolds itself in the pageant of history—a world of seething passions, of loves and hates, of joys and sorrows, of lights and shades, of conflicting aims and interests, of realities and illusions, of ideals true and false; and in that turmoil, that seeming chaos, he discerns, more or less clearly, the real order of things, and he calls on his fellow-men, by

[1] But perhaps the supreme artist is, unknown to himself, something of a prophet and something of a mystic; and if so he can use his own art as an appropriate medium of expression for his vision of reality. For this purpose some arts are more appropriate than others. Poetry, in the stricter but not the strictest sense of the word, is the art through which "philosophy" makes its readiest appeal to the general heart of man. It is possible that music, though it appeals less to thought than to feeling—or perhaps for that very reason—goes beyond poetry in its power of penetrating into the heart of reality. But so far as the conscious quest of wisdom is concerned, the great "poet", whether as seer or revealer, takes precedence of the great "composer".

exhortation and denunciation, to conform to the real order; to bring their lives into line with it; to turn away from the shadows that delude them, and hold fast to the realities that are within—and beyond—their reach. He is, as a rule, in revolt against the dominant tendencies of the age in which he lives, so far at least as these claim to be permanent and authoritative. There is something of the heretic in him, something of the rebel. He fills a conspicuous place in the literature of the world. There has been no great, no genuinely inspired, writer who was not a prophet in some respect and some degree.

The mystic looks inward instead of outward. He believes that the fountain-head of reality is his own true self, and he tries by self-discipline and self-transcendence, by losing self that he may find it, by learning to live in his own depths, to unseal that hidden fountain and bathe his being in its supernal light.[1]

Prophecy and mysticism should never be wholly disjoined. The prophet who has in him no strain of the mystic, who does not draw his inspiration, in part at least, from his inner experiences, will sooner or later grow hard in his own shallow—and ever shallowing—convictions. If he is in deadly earnest, he will become a fanatic, a narrow-minded zealot, a persecutor of dissentient opinion,

[1] The practical side of mysticism will be considered in the next section of this chapter. Here I am thinking of the mystic as a seer rather than a saint.

a ruthless propagandist of what, in the blindness of his intolerance and want of sympathy, he regards as the sum-total of truth.

And the mystic who has in him no strain of the prophet, who is content to live in his own experiences and has no wish to give utterance to these and share them with others, has not, we may be sure, gone deep enough into his own depths. Sooner or later he will become selfish and self-centred; and the Nemesis of this will be the gradual obscuration of his vision of reality and a growing blindness to the inward light—the light which lighteth every man that cometh into this world, and which has not been truly discerned by him who can think of it as in any sense exclusively his own.

When there is a perfect harmony between prophecy and mysticism we have the true philosopher, the whole-hearted lover of wisdom, the inspired teacher who can speak to his fellow-men, not in the jargon of metaphysics, but in the language of poetry, the language which emotion, when it is kindled by vision, finds for itself, the language which comes from the heart and speaks to the heart, and which is therefore independent of time and place, intelligible in all ages and in all lands. This fusion of prophecy and mysticism into a larger unity was characteristic of the spiritual philosophy of Ancient India. For us of the West its typical exponent was Christ. For us Christ was the greatest of mystics and the greatest of prophets. And because he was each of these he was also the greatest of spiritual teachers. So deeply had he sounded the depths of his own being, and so vividly did he live in those depths, that he found there what we are all seeking—the Ultimate Reality which men call God, and which for him was at once his loving Father and his own real self. "I and my Father are one." His recognition of the fatherhood of God, his realization in his own person that the light of love is at the heart of the Universe, filled his heart with a sacred joy which overflowed into inspired poetry when he spoke to his fellow-men. He was not a metaphysician. He was not even a systematic thinker. His philosophy was too large, too free and too intensely alive to be imprisoned in any system. But in spite of centuries of misunderstanding and misrepresentation on the part of those who interpreted him to mankind; in spite of all that system-mongers of various kinds—ecclesiastics, sectaries, theologians, legalists, ceremonialists, literalists and other hyperlogical exploiters—have done to obscure and distort his message, his teaching, which found its consummation and final expression in his death on the cross, still goes to our hearts, still opens our eyes to the inner truth of things, still gives us a vision of reality, is still a trumpet-call to each of us to lead a higher and a nobler life.

And it is open to each of us to verify Christ's

teaching for himself. For his philosophy was intuitional to the core. There was in it no metaphysical word-play, no quasi-scientific marshalling of arguments, no merely logical movement of thought. It was poetry, in the largest and deepest sense of the word—poetry in its inspiration, poetry in its ideas, poetry in its form. And poetry says to each of us, "Take me and try my worth. Try me in your heart. Try me in your life."

In metaphysics of the logical type speculation deliberately transcends or tries to transcend experience, and in doing so precludes itself from appealing to experience in support of its conclusions. If its assumptions are plausible enough to win acceptance from careless or superficial minds, if its reasoning seem to be correct, if the demands of a more or less formal logic have been complied with, it is content with itself and asks for no further proof of its soundness. That its conclusions will have to stand the test of experience is indeed inevitable. But the verdict of experience is one which the logical metaphysician can allow himself to ignore.

In the metaphysics which calls itself empirical the arbitrary limitation of experience to sense-experience makes the appeal to experience, in the wider and deeper sense of the word, meaningless and impossible. Empirical metaphysics is, on its own showing, a branch of physical science; and verification by experience means no more to the has done for mankind is a convincing proof of the truth of Christ's teaching, and of the readiness to discern spiritual truth and welcome it which is latent in the heart of man.

Intuitional philosophy is diffused through the literature of the world. There are few inspired poets who have not in them a strain of the mystic and the prophet. And there is no mystic or prophet who, when the fire is kindled in his heart, does not express himself in the language of poetry. But intuitional philosophy is necessarily unsystematic. There is nothing in it which can be formulated, nothing which can be labelled and pigeon-holed, nothing which we can lay our hands upon when we are at a loss for a clue to the maze of life. What it offers us is the guidance which has its counterpart in inspiration, the guidance which is generated by the vision of a high ideal. What it does not offer us is certitude, scientific or quasi-scientific precision, mental repose. "Wisdom" goes beyond these, and the lover of wisdom must be prepared to resist their allurements. If he will do so, if he will be content to "find peace of mind in infinite unrest", a light, which, as he advances, will become clearer and stronger, will dawn upon his soul.

*The Practical Quest of Wisdom.*—Wordsworth tells us that the "best philosopher" is the "little child", because on him

"those truths do rest
Which we are toiling all our lives to find".

The conception of philosophy which underlies this seeming paradox is, I think, profoundly true. The best philosophy is not that which provides us with a solution of the great problem such as will satisfy our mental curiosity; it is that which teaches us, which inspires us, which helps us to *become* real—which enables us, in other words, to solve the great problem, not by *thinking* our way to the so-called truth of things, but by *seeing* our way, by *feeling* our way, above all by *living* our way, into the very heart of reality. The little child is living, though he does not know it, at the heart of reality. He is in vital contact with ultimate truth.

Let us remind ourselves that philosophy is the love of wisdom, and that wisdom is the guiding light which enables us to steer our way in safety through the dangers and perplexities of life. The "love of wisdom", if it is a genuine love, must needs resolve itself into the quest of wisdom, and the quest of wisdom must needs resolve itself into the quest of reality; for it is from the central flame of Ultimate Reality that the light is shed which irradiates the world.

The quest of reality takes various forms. In metaphysics it is intellectual—an attempt, by dint of hard thinking, to solve the riddle of the Universe, and in and through that solution to grasp the truth of things; in other words, to distinguish reality from illusion at the very fountain-head of Being. That attempt is, as we have seen, foredoomed to failure. As a truth to be grasped by thought, to be surveyed, analysed and formulated, to be presented to consciousness for acceptance or rejection, the ultimately real is a dream from which we shall awake when we have attained to a higher level of life and so got nearer to the heart of reality. The initial assumption that ultimate reality can be brought within the compass of intellectual effort involves a degradation of it in our thought, a narrowing of its scope, a lowering of its level, which stultifies all our attempts to translate the "truth of things" into a system of thought and embody it in a scheme of life.

The poetic quest of reality is much more hopeful. Here the satisfaction that is demanded by the adventurous spirit is emotional, not intellectual. It is taken for granted that the test of reality is in the quality of the feeling that it generates; that contact with reality will be realized as pure and deep emotion which carries with it complete assurance of its own genuineness and worth; that the vision of reality will produce a sense of vital well-being, of being truly alive, an inward and spiritual joy, which will sooner or later overflow into speech and express itself in the language of inspiration, of poetry.

For the rank and file of mankind the language of metaphysics is a meaningless jargon. But even the language of poetry, though it may sometimes awake responsive chords in their hearts and though its indirect influence on their lives may be very great, is on the whole an unfamiliar tongue. Yet the guiding light which we call wisdom is at their service if they will but open their eyes to it. For it is the light of their own inward and spiritual reality, the light which makes each of us a potential "lamp unto himself".

Why is the lamp of wisdom hidden from most of us? Why, if it is not actually hidden, does it shine so often with a faint, flickering light? Because the veil of "self" hangs between us and it; because the familiar, superficial, individual self, self-conscious, self-centred, self-satisfied, is ever trying to pass itself off as the real self; and because we too easily fall victims to its seductions and to the consequent confusion between illusion and reality.

What do we mean by "self"?[1] The word has an immense range of meaning. Let us try to come to terms with the underlying idea. When a living being has become a conscious sharer in the real, the inner, the spiritual life of the world, selfhood has been achieved. The living being has become a living soul, and we speak of him as *man*. The

[1] In this and the three following paragraphs I have borrowed freely from a book which I brought out last year, called *The World of Self or Spirit; A Scheme of Life*, a book in which the problem of *selfhood* is dealt with more fully than is possible within the limits of a section of a chapter.

inner life, as shared in by him, constitutes his self; and his awareness of that inner life, however dim, fitful and otherwise misleading it may be, is what we call his consciousness of self. The approach to selfhood in the ascending scale of life has been gradual, and we cannot say for certain when it reached its goal.

But did it reach its goal? Has it ever reached it? Will it ever reach it? Is self a finished and finite entity, complete in itself, imprisoned in its own individuality, walled off from all other selves, from all other forms of life and from the surrounding world? Our first impulse is to say Yes in answer to this question; and so far as a man yields to that impulse and gives practical expression to his answer he separates himself from his fellows and from the world at large and enters a prison, the walls of which will gradually close in on him who is content to dwell in it.

Our first impulse is to ascribe intrinsic reality to the individual self. But our sense of oneness with our fellow-men through community of interests, through the growing need for co-operation, through sympathy, through love, and of oneness with other forms of life and other planes of being through curiosity and understanding and wonder and admiration—a sense which seems to admit of systematic cultivation and indefinite expansion—gradually undermines the sense of isolation in which too many of us are content to empirical metaphysician than it means to the physicist or the biologist.[1] There are no tests known to science by which the wisdom of a philosophy, or a creed, or a scheme of life, or an ideal, can be detected and measured.

In intuitional philosophy, on the other hand, which is itself the outcome of experience, verification by experience is both permissible and possible, is indeed an essential part of the whole process of thinking. For intuition is critical as well as revelational. It can both discern hidden reality and pass judgment on the account that it gives of its own exploratory work. The two processes are really one. In the act of inspiring and quickening the inner life the seer's vision of reality appeals to the inner life for confirmation of its own authenticity. It follows that in testing its own worth it tests the worth of him to whom it speaks. We see this clearly in the case of Christ. In his teaching we have the high-water mark of intuitional philosophy. We have also an appeal to what is best in human nature, an appeal which evokes what is best, awakes it from the slumber of mere potentiality and quickens it into active life. In the response that he makes to Christ's message each of us passes judgment on it and on himself. What the message

[1] Whether it means as much, or anything like as much, is a question which I cannot help asking, but am not competent to discuss. The empirical metaphysician must justify his claim to the title of metaphysician to his fellow-metaphysicians, and his claim to the title of scientist to his fellow-scientists.

rest. And as the sense of oneness with others grows upon us and the sense of isolation weakens, the idea that self is (in the language of scholastic philosophy) an "absolutely simple substance", and that the individual self is therefore the whole of self, loses its hold upon us and a new conception of self begins to dawn upon our thought.

What form does this conception take? If the inner reality of things, as shared in by us, constitutes the self of each of us, and if that inner reality, that ocean of spiritual life, has no limits, why should we assign limits to the power of sharing in it which we all possess? Again, if there is a gradual approach to selfhood in the worlds of plant and animal life, why should there not be a further ascent in the world of self-conscious life to unknown heights of spirituality? We habitually speak of the lower self and the higher self, of the false self and the true self, of the self which must be lost and the self which must be found, of the self which we must die to and the self which we must live to. Is there not a meaning in these antitheses? And if they have a meaning, do not they suggest to us that the range of self is unlimited, and that the boundaries which our conscious thought assigns to it have no counterpart in reality? The more closely I meditate on this problem the stronger does my conviction become that self is not so much a limited entity as a limitless world.

This was the idea which inspired Christ's great predecessor, the Buddha, and which he embodied in his wonderful scheme of life. He sought to liberate his fellow-men from the "heresy of individuality" and so open a way of life to them, a way of escape from the fetters of illusion, a way of approach to the reality which was hidden in each of them and which for each of them was his own real self.

We need not go into the details of Buddha's scheme of life. It was, in the fullest sense of the word, a *practical* scheme. It was to be judged by its fruits, not by its metaphysical antecedents. No great thinker was ever so impatient as he was of metaphysical subtleties and sophistries. The theories which interested the metaphysicians of his day, and which they disputed about till they lost their bearings and their tempers, had no interest for him, except so far as he regarded them as hindrances to the higher life. What he said of one of them, he said of all: "This theory is a jungle, a wilderness, a puppet-show, a writhing, and a fetter." Knowledge of reality was to be won, not by metaphysical speculation, but by conduct, by right action, by inward and spiritual effort. He said to each and all of us: "If you would win deliverance from sorrow and suffering, you must gain the knowledge of reality which will enable you to transform the whole range of your desires. If you would gain knowledge of reality, you must try to *become* real. You cannot *think* your way to reality, for the way of thought in such matters loses itself at last in a quicksand of words. Few of you can enjoy at the outset of life the *vision* of reality, though that may come at last to those who have earned it by their lives. But you can all, if you will, *live* your way into the heart of reality. Live the life of self-discipline, self-development and self-transcendence, and you will find in the depths of self the guiding light which the sage is ever seeking, the light which, as reality, for ever enfolds you and, as truth, for ever eludes your thought. The truth of things is not a riddle to be guessed but an ideal to be followed. Follow it, and you will become wiser than the wisest, for you will gain an ever deepening insight into the meaning and purpose of life."

The sum and substance of this teaching is that the pathway to the wisdom which philosophy loves and seeks is the pathway to knowledge of reality, and that the pathway to knowledge of reality is the pathway to one's own real self. It follows that the "best philosopher" is he who loses self that he may find self, who dies to self that he may live to self, who subdues the lower desires that he may awake the higher desires, who strives unceasingly to bring his life, rather than his thought, into harmony with the inner truth of things. This is the life of virtue, of righteousness, of moral goodness. It is open to all of us.

If we will try it we shall realize, each for himself, that the philosophy which it embodies is true. Even at its highest level, the level of holiness (in the sense of spiritual wholeness), of heroism, of saintliness, it is not beyond our reach.

But mankind must have its leaders in the great adventure of living; and there is a life which all may look up to, revere and profit by, but which few may lead. When the poet has lost himself in the saint, when "vision" has been deepened, strengthened and clarified by self-discipline, by spiritual austerity, by unswerving devotion to an inward ideal, we get the mystic, the greatest of all pioneers in the quest of reality, the man whose experiences so far transcend those of ordinary men that they seem to belong to another world. But the wonders and glories which unveil themselves to mystic vision are transcendental only in the sense that in them the world of our experience enlarges its own limits, transcends itself from within. The mystic, if we measure him by our own normal standards, is a subject for incredulity and ridicule. But his mission is to expose the inadequacy of our normal standards, to force us to look beyond them, to fill us with a divine discontent. In mysticism the two great streams of intuitional philosophy, the speculative and the practical, meet and mingle, each at its fullest flood. In the mystic the seer and the saint are one.

Metaphysical philosophy makes no attempt to verify its conclusions. It could not do so if it would, and it would not if it could. When metaphysicians quarrel they try to pick holes in one another's arguments. They try to prove that there are logical flaws in them, that the reasoning process as a whole is unsound. They do not, they cannot appeal against one another to experience.

Intuitional philosophy, on its speculative side, appeals to the general heart of men and is willing to abide by its verdict. But to interpret that verdict is very difficult. Temperaments differ, sentiments differ, opinions differ, aims and interests differ; and each of us is all too ready to read into the teaching of history his own prejudices and convictions. Yet the fact remains that the conclusions of intuitional philosophy are being continually tested by experience; that the exponents of that philosophy—the poet and the prophet—are ready to profit by the results of the testing process, ready to modify their respective outlooks on life in response to the reaction of experience on their teaching, ready to assimilate the subtle influence on their minds of

> "the prophetic soul,
> Of the wide world dreaming on things to come".

Practical philosophy each of us can test for himself. The test may be life-long, but it is as simple from one point of view as it is difficult from another. If a man will order his own life in accordance with the first principles of a particular philosophy, he will sooner or later be able to test its worth. If on the whole and in the long run his manner of living brings him inward well-being, and that sense of inward well-being which we call happiness, he will know that the philosophy which is embodied and expressed in his conduct is fundamentally sound, that it is true for him, and therefore has in it elements of truth for all men. And the more steadily he keeps its precepts in view, the clearer will be his insight into the conception of reality that underlies it, the truer will be his own vision of reality, and the better will he be able to avoid the quicksands of illusion. For the intuition of reality, like every other sense, grows by being exercised. There is a gain to it in every act of self-discipline, in every act of obedience to a warning voice, in every response to the appeal of one's better self. Knowledge prepares the way for right action, and right action prepares the way for the further advance of knowledge; and in the mutual interplay of knowledge and action there is more of true wisdom than in all the complexities and profundities of speculative thought. The life of simple, homely goodness, of kindness, unselfishness, tolerance, temperance, is for most of us the surest road to reality; for such a life is in itself a gradual withdrawal of the darkening screen of self, a gradual unveiling of the inner light.

> "Far has he gone whose feet
> tread down one fond offence."

"The pure in heart", not the mighty in intellect, "shall see God". For the pure in heart has escaped from the prison of self into the light of love; and the light of love is the light of innermost reality, the light of the presence of God.

# CONCLUSION

How does intuitional philosophy, whether poetic or practical, tend to interpret the universe? Is there any main current of belief which runs through and takes up into itself the many partial solutions—convictions rather than conclusions—which that philosophy offers us? I think there is. Nay, I am very sure that there must be. In separating itself from metaphysics, whether logical, or empirical, or popular, intuitional philosophy strikes out a path for itself which is not the less distinctive because it is, in a sense, as wide as the world. It has its own assumption about reality; and in every assumption about reality a whole philosophy is potentially present. It seeks wisdom through experience, not through sense-experience only or even mainly, but through the all-embracing, self-transcending experience which meets us at every turn, which grows with our growth, and through which we establish contact with the possibilities as well as the actualities of existence.

Now the world of which we have experience, the world in which we live, the world to whose ceaseless and ubiquitous pressure we respond with *feeling*, is a world of Becoming, a world of Life. And wherever there is life there is growth; and wherever there is growth there is continuous transition from *is* to *is not*, and from *is not* to *is*.

The growing organism is for ever becoming what it was not and is not, but what it really is; for ever finding itself by losing itself, affirming itself by contradicting itself, keeping true to itself by disowning itself, preserving its identity by changing it. Is it not the same with the growing or evolving world? In the world around us, in ourselves, in every exponent of the law of growth, there is unceasing movement towards what the thing really is, towards higher and ever higher levels of reality. When maturity has been reached decay begins. But in ourselves and in the world around us maturity has never been reached, and, so far as we can see, will never be reached. The goal recedes as we approach it, recedes into the darkness of its own ever-increasing light. And this eternal elusiveness, this capacity for limitless self-transcendence, is the very hall-mark of its reality, the very proof that life has a meaning and a purpose, that what it pursues is no flying phantom, but the most substantial of all realities—the unattainable Ideal, the eternal Beyond.

*The Ideal is the Real.* In the logic of Being ideality or self-transcendence is the proof of unreality, the proof that reality has not yet been reached. In the logic of Becoming, the logic of a world which is a living paradox, ideality is the proof of reality, the proof that the movement is real beyond all reality—real, because it has not reached and will never reach its goal.

This is the assumption about reality which is at the heart of intuitional philosophy, whether poetic or practical. It is an assumption, and therefore in a sense a begging of the question. But it is an assumption which is ever generated by the pressure of experience and which is ever verifying itself by an appeal to the test of experience. It is no mere theory, content with itself because it has been correctly deduced from what passes as a self-evident principle, and therefore disdaining the support which congruity with experience (if that could be proved) would give it. It is no mere formula, to be learnt by heart and recited—and forgotten. It is the supreme postulate of man's higher thought, the mainspring of his higher life. The conviction that the Ideal is the Real has been the inspiration of the Poet—the Maker, the Seer —in all ages, and the conviction that the way to the Ideal is the way of self-transcendence has been the inspiration of the Saint in all ages, besides being the master motive to virtue in its homelier and less heroic forms.

The Ideal is the Real. And the headquarters of ideality, and therefore of reality, are in *self*. Intuitional philosophy centres in the supreme intuition, in the intuition of self, in the revelation of self to self. It is on acceptance of this revelation as the bedrock of truth that its own claim to recognition is based, and that its whole theory of things is hinged. And it is in the quest of the ideal self, as the fountain-head of the Inward Light, that it finds itself both as a search for wisdom and as a scheme of life.

Intuitional philosophy has a logic of its own. This is, I think, indisputable. We cannot elaborate its logic into a system. We can scarcely begin to formulate its rules. But of its reality, and even of its efficacy, there can be no doubt. Anyone who has ever been aware, in any degree, of the working of his mind when he is trying to think out, trying to feel his way into the heart of—(either expression might be used)—a difficult philosophical problem, will tell you that he was doing far more than registering a succession of emotional impressions. He was following out, subconsciously, but not the less carefully and consistently, a line of argumentative thought, examining a succession of arguments as they presented themselves to him, growing out of one another—rejecting some, accepting and developing others, and arriving at last at a conclusion, paradoxical perhaps in form, which would have presented itself to him, had he not for once in a way turned a feeble and flickering searchlight on the workings of his mind, as a more or less instinctive conviction.

In such a case one feels that the reasoning has been done for one quite as much as by one, and this feeling sets one thinking as to the nature and origin of logic. What is logic, I sometimes say to myself, but the rising up into human consciousness of the *reason*—the law-making, law-enforcing and law-administering power—which rules all the realms of existence and directs all the processes of Nature (in the widest sense of that much abused word); which enables man, as it reveals itself to him, to trust Nature, to place entire confidence in her objective veracity; and which hides itself at last, as we try to follow it out towards its fountain-head, at the very heart of the universe, as the innermost core of reality, lost in its own inviolable light. As it rises into consciousness reason accommodates itself to our mental limitations by shedding (so to speak) more and more of the subtlety and complexity and swift sagacity which are of its essence. It follows that the nearer it comes to the surface of consciousness, the less is its capacity for directing the processes of thought and things, and the lower is the level of existence which is amenable to its control. When it rises at last to the surface-level of consciousness, when we are able to formulate its rules and consciously work by these, we have the logic of the logician; the logic which is most at home when its subject-matter is most abstract and therefore farthest removed from reality, but which is also at home, though in a lesser degree, with what is one stage nearer to reality, with the material framework of the world. It is to this development of logic, which betrays its relative impotence by its submission to systematization and formulation, by its allowing itself to be imprisoned in handbooks and other treatises, that the metaphysician would entrust the solution of the largest, most complex and most intangible of all problems. Or rather it is to the human intellect, working under the guidance of this rushlight, that he would assign the greatest of all adventures, the attempt to understand the universe, to know reality.

Let the metaphysician fence, if he will, with his fellow-experts. Let him parry their thrusts and count his own hits. The lover of wisdom will look elsewhere for guidance. He will try to widen the range and increase the penetrative power of consciousness. He will try to lift into its light levels of mental activity which are still in darkness. He will try to shed its rays into the deeper darkness of man's psychic life. He will try (to change our imagery) to raise to the surface of consciousness the waters of wisdom which are slumbering in the dark recesses of the soul. For this is the real meaning, the real value, of the attempt to think things out. If it is made by the whole man, heart co-operating with mind, instinct with intellect, vision with logic, it will set in motion the reservoirs of subconscious reason, of unsystematized thought, which are hidden in each of us; making demands on these which will be felt and responded to far and wide, till at last some ripple of their movement will reach the very headsprings of the "buried life".

The object of the philosopher's quest is wisdom. Where is wisdom to be found? Not in any system of thought. Not in any assumption about reality. Not in any formulated creed. But at the heart of the universe, at the heart of the heart of man. Yet each of us must have his philosophy of life, his vision of reality, his unformulated creed. Metaphysics dreams of a formulated philosophy, elaborated by specialists, which, like the Binomial Theorem, is binding upon all men because it is intrinsically and indisputably true. Intuitionism sets each of us free to have his own philosophy, his own creed, to be a lamp unto himself. It is as tolerant on principle as metaphysics is the reverse; and being tolerant it makes for unity in the diversity of beliefs and opinions, and therefore for peace and good will.

Each of us must have his own creed, his own way of responding to the pressure of his environment, to the challenge of his existence. And I, for one, have mine. It is the creed of an intuitionist, of one who refuses to specialize in philosophy, refuses to undergo any training for the task of high thinking but that which is given by experience of life; of one who believes that the whole man, working by methods which are best known to his inner self, must take up the burden of wrestling with the supreme problem.

This creed, the creed of my heart, may be set forth in five short sentences, each of which is a paradox, for it is only in the language of paradox that an unformulated creed will allow itself to be formulated[1]:—

> Becoming is of the essence of being.
> Ideality is of the essence of reality.
> Self-transcendence is of the essence of self-identity.
> "Effort and expectation and desire" are of the essence of inward peace.
> The "something evermore about to be" is the thing that really is.

Behind these articles of belief there is a faith so large and so deep that it refuses to be limited by expression, and so sure of itself that it is well content to remain unexpressed. For

> "He is unknown to those who think they know,
> But known to those who know they know Him not".

With this paradox of paradoxes, philosophy, as I understand the word, finally parts company with metaphysics.

[1] I have elsewhere ventured to define paradox as "the appeal of imagination to imagination behind the back of reason, in order to save reason from itself".